Fast-Growth
Strategies

Fast-Growth Strategies

How to Maximize Profits From Start-Up Through Maturity

Mack Hanan

McGraw-Hill Book Company

New York   St. Louis   San Francisco   Auckland
Bogotá   Hamburg   Johannesburg   London   Madrid
Mexico   Milan   Montreal   New Delhi   Panama
Paris   São Paulo   Singapore
Sydney   Tokyo   Toronto

Library of Congress Cataloging-in-Publication Data

Hanan, Mack.
  Fast-growth strategies.

  Includes index.
  1. Corporate planning.   2. Corporate profits.
3. Sales management.   I. Title.
HD30.28.H363   1987   658.4   86-21673
ISBN 0-07-025972-0

1 2 3 4 5 6 7 8 9 0   DOC/DOC   8 9 3 2 1 0 9 8 7 6

ISBN 0-07-025972-0

The editors for this book were William A. Sabin and Nancy Young,
the designer was Naomi Auerback, and the production supervisor
was Teresa F. Leaden. It was set in Baskerville by Braun-Brumfield, Inc.
Printed and bound by R. R. Donnelley & Sons Company.

To Tom Watson

Who shared with me the vision
He gave IBM of growth: not to grow
Corporate size or market share
Or computer performance but
Customer profits,
So that while all who competed against
This vision searched for excellence,
Sought competitive advantage, pursued
Megatrends, and claimed the vital difference,
IBM made its customers grow and,
As a result, grew itself.

Contents

Fast-Growth Strategies

PART 1
The Growth Vision

1
Introduction

When major corporations try to grow internally, they fail far more often than they succeed. They fail to advocate growth. They decline its sponsorship. They fail to reward growth. They underestimate the ignition point of business growers. They fail even to buy good growth, typically acquiring businesses so closely related to their own that they are also mature or will soon become so. At the other extreme, they bring in entrepreneurial businesses that are based on futuristic technologies that they do not understand, cannot manage, and frequently suffocate. Even when growth comes knocking on their door, they turn away from it.

Chester Carlson and his "long march" in search of sponsors for the copying process that eventually became xerography is a twentieth-century symbol of the corporate inability to recognize growth. Only when Joseph Wilson saw the potential of Carlson's copier did it take off. Yet for every Joseph Wilson, there were dozens who, like even Thomas Watson at IBM, thanked Carlson for coming by but said, "No thank you." Nonetheless, it was the same Watson who was able to see the potential of the computer when Ralph Cordiner of General Electric could not. Cordiner took GE into data processing too late and never got it out of the red. IBM has made its fortune on it. But GE was nevertheless able to see how a generation of profits could be made from electrical appliances while Westinghouse's Gwilyn Price could not.

The ability to envision growth, let alone convert that vision into a commercially profitable business, has always been unevenly distributed. In 1913, Lee De Forest was hauled from his laboratory into court and charged with fraudulent use of the mails. His crime was to try to sell stock in his Radio Telephone Company, which was commercializing his invention of the audion broadcasting tube. The United States attorney

3

summarized his prosecution by charging, "De Forest has said in many newspapers and over his signature that it would be possible to transmit the human voice across the Atlantic before many years. Based on these absurd and deliberately misleading statements, the misguided public has been persuaded to purchase stock in his company."

David Sarnoff was persuaded more by De Forest than by the United States attorney. He saw a growth business in radio. He tried to interest Eldridge Johnson in it, since Johnson was already in the business of sound transmission as president of the Victor Talking Machine Company. But the radio was a different sort of talking machine than the Victrola. Although Johnson could hear Sarnoff's radio, he could not see it as a growth opportunity. Sarnoff decided to go it alone. When he had made millions from radio, his RCA bought out Victor and operated it as a division.

Three years before De Forest's trial, in 1910, a business grower named Will Durant had gathered together Buick, Oldsmobile, Cadillac, and seventeen other automobile companies. Seeking funds to continue his agglomeration, he suggested to J. P. Morgan that automobiles would soon become an important factor in American life. Morgan, a railroad financier at the time, was busy protecting his New York, New Haven & Hartford Railroad by buying up potentially competitive trolley lines and steamboat companies at highly inflated prices. As events turned out, his concerns were unwarranted. Durant's automobiles were destined to dispose of these competitors anyway in just a few years' time in the same way they were to supersede the railroad itself. But Morgan's reaction to Durant's "crackpot suggestion" was to have him forcibly escorted from the Morgan offices.

Yet it was Henry Ford and not Will Durant who saw the true growth of the automobile. He became so transfixed with his vision of putting an automobile into every garage that he failed to sense his market's growing need for more than just one model in one color at one price. Nor could he see the automobile's inevitable effect on the growth of consumer credit. By concentrating on the revolution he had wrought, he blinded himself to its evolution. After a run of 20 years, the popularity of his Model T went into decline as Alfred Sloan at General Motors began to offer multiple models in many price ranges with consumer credit to boot.

Morgan's negative reaction to the automobile, like Watson's limited view of Chester Carlson's copying machine, is simply a continuation of the process by which human minds in business replicate the act of denying growth by "laughing at Fulton." Up to recently, this has been an affordable, if lamentable, luxury. It will no longer be so.

Growth—growth at a high rate of profit generation—will become our increasingly inescapable mandate. The reason is simple: There is no other way to accumulate sufficient capital. Either it will come from internally produced growth profits or it will not come at all. Without a high rate of growth of new S-curves, the speeded-up telescoping of business life cycles will cause the profit streams of mainstay businesses to evaporate. It is hard to argue against the need for growth when the alternative is capital starvation. But there is no way to grow with the shopworn strategies of the pre-1980 years.

The paradox of our past methods of growth management can be summed up in a single statement: We have been objectives rich but strategy poor.

When we dedicate ourselves to growth, we typically set objectives that few if any of our traditional businesses have ever achieved. How can we expect to seize them in a new business? If we reach them, how can we expect to be able to manage them—where will we find managers who have proven themselves able to hold the road at a 20 percent to 30 percent rate of growth?

How can we make growth like this? How can we manage it? These questions are the major management issues of our time. Businesses that answer them possess growth capability for the business environment of the decades between now and the year 2000. Others will say, in hindsight, as Du Pont said looking over its shoulder in 1980, "We didn't know where the end of the rainbow was." Such businesses will go on asking irrelevant questions that they believe still have major bearing on their profitability. They will want to know how large a market is, how homogeneous its demand base will be, and how lasting a franchise they can enjoy. "Where does it fit our mainstream business?" they will ask, even though for many of them the fact that a fit does indeed exist is *prima facie* evidence that there is no basis for growth.

Many of these companies will fall off the S-curve—the profitable phase of their life cycle will end abruptly—and they will drop into the profitless pit of slow growth or no growth maturity. The more optimistic they are, the more likely they are to believe that this is merely the first step. Unfortunately, there is rarely a second one. For these companies, a new growth drive is not merely desirable. It is imperative. To continue to do more of what they have been doing, but to do better at its strategic planning, is merely to rearrange the deck chairs.

How many other companies will pass the end of the rainbow between now and the year 2000? It is virtually certain that every business whose profits flow from the volume sales of mature commodity-type products and whose scientific and marketing technologies are obsolete or obsolescent will be in trouble.

What will bail them out? The learning curve theory is dead. The strategic planning process has failed as a growth tool. The product life cycle is in rapid decline, undergoing excruciating pressure. Growth models being advanced by unsophisticated practitioners are inherently flawed. How can we grow into growth?

Death of the Learning Curve Theory

Throughout the 1960s and 1970s, companies en masse fell prey to the learning curve theory. The curve theory, sometimes referred to as the experience curve, exalted volume. Decrease cost per unit by increasing the number of units, the theory said. The resulting low marginal cost will enable competitors to be underpriced. The resulting price cut would gain the high market share that causes high profits. To be the low-cost producer and the high market-share holder at one and the same time was to be unbeatable.

At B. F. Goodrich, it was believed that "the best way to run a tire company was to make as many tires as possible." At U. S. Steel, it was gospel that "when we make the tonnage we make the dollars." Tons, gallons, yards, units of all sorts became the prime business objective. No matter how low their margins, enough of them would add up to profits. For a while they did, until the rate of decay began to run ahead of the rate of growth. From that moment on it has become increasingly clear what the curve's true learning value really is: to teach us that markets, not manufacturing processes, are the true sources of profit.

From the 1970s on, markets have been undergoing dramatic change. They are becoming smaller, and based on highly specialized needs. Their demand for customer-tailored benefits has become the key to their segmentation. At the same time, pressure from new technologies has acted to telescope product life cycles and drive them down toward their break-even points. The combination of smaller markets and shorter commercial lives has conspired against long low-cost production runs. Another change in the nature of demand adds to the conspiracy. Information is becoming a higher percentage of the total composition and cost of many product systems, either in the form of software or applications consultation. Information-dependent systems are less amenable to cost reduction because there is less manufacturing cost to reduce and little learning curve effect, since it is always customized.

No matter how hard they tried, companies that had bought into the learning curve could not lower production costs enough, increase productivity enough, or sell enough at high margins to make profits.

Because they had emphasized volume production and sales of commodity products, low margins became their curse.

Experiences like Sperry Univac's have been common. Univac shipped 40,000 computer terminals one year but earned only the same amount of revenue as it had on the 25,000 units it had turned out the year before. Edward Telling of Sears has written the learning curve obituary. "Market share really doesn't have anything to do with generating profit. It can be a very expensive way to dissipate profits." Sometimes the relationship is directly opposed. The greater the market share, the smaller the profits. To be the market leader can be the worst situation. Shrinkage is the only solution until a new strategy can be formulated around innovative benefits, vertical market segmentation, and high-margin selling.

It has been said that infatuation with the learning curve has helped many industries stretch out their ability to commercialize aging mainstay technologies and that this has been its most notable accomplishment. If so, it is regrettable. A more profitable use for the resources allocated to extend senescent technologies and expand market shares would have been to invest them in researching emergent technologies and novel market needs, supporting new sciences and concentrating on high-value high-margin brands that can command a high rate of return.

In the long run, the learning curve theory defeated growth for its most ardent practitioners by forcing them into low-margin commodity businesses in which the costs of supporting their volume and the progressive erosion of their price-cut margins made growth profits impossible. The learning curve has been revealed as the antithesis of growth—a commodity curve.

As the Boston Consulting Group, former propagandists for the learning curve theory, now admit as they echo Sears, Sperry, and others, "the relationship between relative market share and profitability doesn't hold as much significance anymore." The cash cows are giving sour milk. In the symbolic language of the Group, learning curve theory has become a "dog," ready for divestment.

The Strategic
Planning Failure

Strategic planning attempts to insure cost-effective business continuity. Because growth is discontinuous and cost ineffective, it conflicts head-on with planning that must protect past successes by developing existing markets from current asset bases. The growth that is provided by strategic plans is incremental growth, the annual enhancement of a past year's earnings. True growth, on the other hand, is represented by break-through earnings at a minimum 20 percent compounded annual rate.

There are several reasons why strategic planning fails to produce break-through growth:

1. Strategic plans depend on the life-cycle state of the mainstream technologies that support a business. If these base sciences are mature, they are probably incapable of commercializing products that can command a premium unit price based on their ability to deliver premium value. Strategic plans foster volume production of commodity products, place emphasis on their price-performance benefits, and devote significant concern to competitive comparisons. Growth plans, by way of contrast, watch the markets more than they preoccupy themselves with competition and rely on high-margin branded products to produce their earnings objectives.

2. Strategic plans start from a self-assay of corporate strengths and weaknesses. Companies that forbid their bookkeepers from auditing their own books suspend their disbelief when it comes to allowing top and middle managers to evaluate their own growth assets. These managers respond by assigning all their existing capabilities to strengths and everything else—especially capabilities their business has never needed—to weakness. They then proceed to plan growth based on their strengths. This steers growth into directly related types of business that require similar strengths based on similar technologies and markets. The bias for declining margins is built in.

3. Strategic plans attempt to balance a business. They try to allocate "something for everybody," giving a fair share of company resources to each line and—within lines—to each function. Sometimes a growing operation will get more cash. At other times it will be milked to provide funds for laggards in an equalizing manner. Growth plans are unbalanced. They are concentrated on only a few businesses. They emphasize only the functions that can make the greatest contribution to rapid earnings flow: marketing and product development. They make no attempt to equalize. Quite the opposite, they deliberately distort operational staffing and resourcing to favor growth contribution. In the same way they concentrate on specific products or services to the exclusion of a fully balanced line, on specific distribution channels and advertising media, on specific regions, and on serving only specific market segments.

4. Strategic plans begin with this year and attempt to plan forward.

Growth plans begin with the third or fifth year out and plan backward to the current year. They start with growth rather than trying to forecast it. They act on an as-if basis: as if growth objectives have already occurred. Then they go back year by year and ask *what must have had to happen* to achieve this year's growth contribution. Instead of trying to "strategize"—that is, to forecast what may quite possibly or most probably happen—growth plans analyze what "had to have happened" and how it must have happened so that growth objectives could be achieved. They apply logical deduction. Even more to the point is that they assume major growth. The discontinuity of growth is factory engineered into the planning process.

The strategies in a strategic plan are most often concerned with the orderly evolutionary development of a business to which a company is already committed. This is their context for growth. If they follow the learning curve theory, short-term productivity will be squeezed into some products and costs will be temporarily squeezed out of others. Either way, profits can be improved. But cost controls and productivity increases in traditional business lines are defensive strategies that signal market maturity, not growth. If they are funded at the expense of new opportunities, they may be signs of management immaturity as well.

Strategic planning suffers from two maladies. One is the "Frenchy's Chinese Oasis" problem of trying to be all things to all customers and ending up being nothing compelling to any of them. The other is strategic planning's romance with contingencies.

A true growth plan must have a way of dealing with contingencies. The best way is to rule them out, substituting instead the bedrock secret of growth, which is commitment to concentration. Contingencies forgive commitment. They announce a lack of requisite faith in the most likely way to grow. They suggest that the managers of growth have quit early on their homework to rule out pernicious contraries from their database or that they have failed to exert sufficient pressure on their assumptions to reduce the number and narrow the range of guesses about the future.

A contingent plan for growth is no plan for growth. The best growth planning starts out with a mix of 80 percent or more factual data and 20 percent or fewer assumptions. As assumptions become progressively transformed into data, the fact base grows. As it undergoes change, the stragegy mix must be automatically altered in response. When strategies change, objectives must be revised. All the while, there is a single plan. It avoids the Chinese Contingency Syndrome.

In 1971, a plot was made to slay Mao Zedong. Mao's special train was first to be attacked with flamethrowers and 40-millimeter bazookas. Because the train was armored and well defended, there were reservations about how well this approach would work. As a result, four contingencies were planned:

1. As the first contingency, the Shuofang railway bridge over which the train was scheduled to pass was to be dynamited.
2. As a further contingency, the train was next to be bombed from the air.
3. In the event the train was still able to proceed, the oil depot near the Shanghai railroad station was to be blown up, taking the train with it.
4. Finally, a member of Mao's special bodyguard had been bribed to shoot Mao when he got off the train in Shanghai.

The plan to slay Mao failed. He got off the train at Shanghai according to his own plan. The plotters' plan failed so completely that even the existence of a plan to assassinate Chairman Mao was not known for several years. Yet to the very last, the planners continued to believe in the law of averages rather than the law of concentration.

The Product Life-Cycle Decline

In the past, growth has been regarded as the first stage following market entry in the business life cycle. At some distant future point it would phase into maturity and finally decline. This discrete one-two-three sequence is illustrated by the traditional curve of normal distribution shown in Figure 1.1. Whether such a curve ever existed in the real world is problematic. Even if it did, it is far more certain that it will rarely if ever be seen again.

From now on, the baseline of virtually every product life cycle will be drastically foreshortened. The former rounded curve is becoming saw-toothed, bobtailed primarily by technological innovations and changing market needs. This reduces significantly the amount of marketable time available to recover a product's up-front investment and make easy marginal dollars by coasting down a prolonged falling slope of the curve. If true growth is to take place, it must get started early and fast and then climb rapidly so it can dwell high and long.

Along with the telescoping of the life cycle's time frame is the compression of the two phases of maturity and decline into one mature phase. The new two-phase curve and the tight relationship it imposes on the volume and time boundaries of growth profits are shown in Figure 1.2. It is notable for its pinched shape and reduced number of phases. Its most significant aspect, however, is the representation it makes that growth does not blend into maturity. Instead, *maturity is contained within growth.* No wonder its onset is so gradual that it is hardly ever recognized until too late.

If sales growth is mistaken for true growth, as long as the sales curve is rising it will be assumed that growth is still taking place and that maturity is being deferred. But when a proper indicator of growth is used as the criterion, the presence of maturity is surprisingly revealed even as volume and share points continue to rise and market leadership

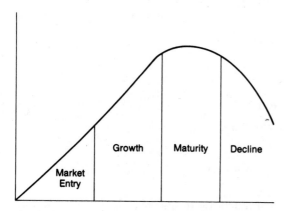

Figure 1.1. Traditional life-cycle curve.

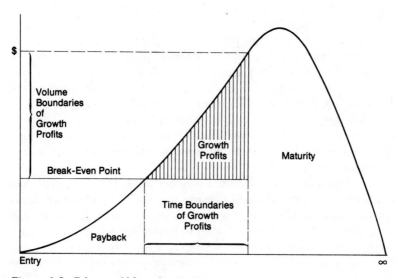

Figure 1.2. Telescoped life-cycle curve.

becomes more firmly entrenched. In this regard, the best index of growth is *the rate of earnings growth.*

In the growth phase, rate of earnings grows progressively. A typical minimum hurdle is a 20 percent compounded annual rate. If the earnings growth rate suddenly stabilizes, a business is sending out an early warning signal that it may be becoming mature. When the growth rate declines, it is almost certain that maturity has occurred no matter what one-time nonrecurrent causes are alleged to explain it.

Over the 1970 to 1979 decade, IBM's annual rate of earnings growth averaged 13.5 percent. Suddenly, in 1979, it showed its first decline in 30 years. IBM put forth seven one-time nonrecurrent causes to explain it:

1. Inflation-based cost increases

2. High interest costs

3. Economic softness

4. Aggressive competitive pricing

5. Unfavorable currency exchange rates

6. New plant start-up costs

7. Slowed growth of major customers

All of these events were real. Each, no doubt, had made a contribution to IBM's decline. But the central reason was none of the above. Maturity had set in. Growth had been ovetaken by decay.

Every rate of growth contains within it a rate of decay. Every growth curve harbors its own genetic code that predetermines its end point. Decay is insidious. Just as high profits ripen, their erosion is forecast. In this sense, maximum profits always terminate prematurely; that is, well in advance of maturity. In Figure 1.3, line B-D represents the decay curve. When it overtakes the growth curve A-C, it will become the backslope of the life cycle. Two strategies can arrest decay. One is to extend the up-slope. This can be accomplished by adroit growth management. The second option is to turn the down-slope around, giving a rebirth to the life cycle by bringing the business back into a growth mode.

The decay process is insidious but it is not invisible. The concurrent fall in profits with the continued rise in sales is the best clue that decay has set in and is accelerating. Figure 1.4 shows a typical relationship between sales and profits as a business moves up the growth curve. Through year 3, the business is still in a growth mode. But the handwriting is on the wall. By year 3, a new growth curve had better be in the works. By year 4, it may be too late.

Flawed Growth Models

Commodity business experience fixates its practitioners on competition. Yet growth is not found in competition—it is found in markets. When commodity practitioners can no longer cost-justify their nth successive marginal difference over their competitors or hold their price points against them, they try to grow the ungrowable with nongrowth strategies. They seek still one more competitive product advantage even though it will be quickly neutralized by imitative competition. They pursue competitive difference to lessen price sensitivity. Simultaneously, their competitors do likewise. The end result is a renewed parity but at a higher cost.

Because commodity practitioners are volume based and product driven, the skill of premium unit pricing for vertical specialty markets is outside their expertise. Through matrices and triads, they express a distorted view of the growth universe that demonstrates why they fail—why they must fail—and how their commodity heritage exerts a deadening bias against growth. Three figures will reveal their thought processes about growth.

The matrix in Figure 1.5 suggests that there are four types of industries. Each type supposedly offers a different number of ways, ranging from many to few, to achieve competitive advantage. In reality,

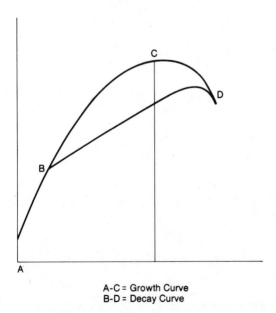

A-C = Growth Curve
B-D = Decay Curve

Figure 1.3. Rate of decay versus rate of growth.

three of the industry types are ungrowable. A volume industry is the same as a nonspecialized industry, which is the same as a stalemated industry. All of them are mature commodity businesses. Competitive advantage can only be achieved by a "specialization" industry, the sole potential category for growth on the matrix.

The matrix in Figure 1.6 is actually Figure 1.5 with eyeshadow. It once again suggests that there are four types of industries. Each type supposedly offers options to counteract price sensitivity through the creation of a perceived competitive difference. In reality, three of the industries are ungrowable: sell for less based on price and/or perfor-

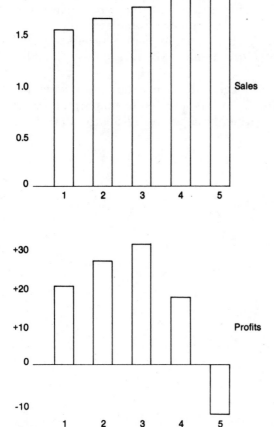

Figure 1.4. Sales-profit relationship from growth to maturity.

mance, spend little on little quality, and commodities, which are simply different ways of describing identical mature businesses. Perceived difference can only be offered by a "specialty" business.

Figure 1.7 is the illegitimate child of Figures 1.5 and 1.6. This triad suggests that there are three types of industries: a cost-leadership commodity industry, a quality-differentiated industry, and a specialty market segment. In reality, two of these industries are brand businesses that can be grown. Cost-based standardized businesses are ungrowable commodities.

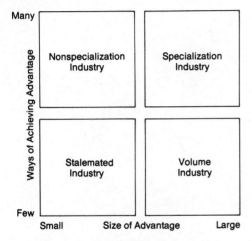

Figure 1.5. Competitive advantage matrix.

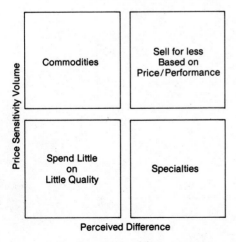

Figure 1.6. Cost reduction-customer value matrix.

These exhibits and their variants, deviants, and adaptations unwittingly say the same thing. For growth purposes, there are only two business classifications. One is commodity businesses that cannot be endowed with superior growth. The other is brand or brandable businesses that can be grown.

Brand and commodity businesses generally exist in an inverse relationship of their price and volume, as the Hanan Slope shows in Figure 1.8. Brand businesses, or rebranded businesses that have been turned around from commodity status, can command growth margins at lower,

Figure 1.7. Generic strategy triad.

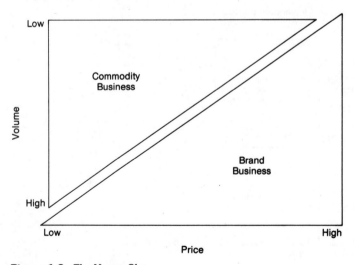

Figure 1.8. The Hanan Slope.

more cost-efficient volumes. That is why they can produce premium profits.

The lesson from the Hanan Slope is clear. There are not four types of growth businesses nor are there three nor two. There is only one. If we brand a business, we can grow it. Otherwise we cannot. All the matrices and triads in the world will do us no good.

Growing into the Growth Process

Is there an ideal growth business? There is, but it remains an ideal because its characteristics are virtually impossible to achieve. Nonetheless, they are worth keeping in mind because it is a constant challenge to see how close we can come to them:

1. A near-monopoly that, like Xerox and Polaroid, can dominate a market because of patents

2. A business whose earnings from sales represent a large proportion of total sales revenues; where, for example, a 20 percent increase in sales can yield a 50 percent increase in net income

3. A business that can grow relatively independently of the economic cycle

4. A business that has a consistently high rate of inquiries and incoming and repeat orders

5. A business that is in a field about which few brokerage reports are written

6. A business that is dependent on management talent

How can we more nearly approach the ideal? We will never reach it by traditional management strategies that deal with businesses whose rates of growth certify them as being at rest. A business at rest tends to remain at rest. A business in a growth mode tends to grow. The best way—perhaps the only way—to grow is to start the process of growth. There is no substitute for doing something. To plan growth and do nothing more simply grows the planning process. *The only way to grow a business is to grow the business.*

There is a proven process for growth. There is also a proven process for nongrowth. The nongrowth process, in common with so many things that do not work, is so much easier than growth. Therefore, it is so much more popular. It proceeds from the belief that growth has only two prerequisites: money and universal participation in coming up with ideas for investing it. Management announces the money and its expectation that people, like a frenzy of spermatozoa, will flock toward it. A typical announcement reads like this:

> Growth is the key to the vitality of our company. The development of new products and services, and the acquisition of new businesses, are necessary to give us the revenue and earnings growth that will provide more opportunities for personal growth for all of us. Accordingly, I am establishing a growth management council (GMC). The purpose of the council, which I will chair, is to stimulate innovation and secure effective implementation of internal starts, acquisitions, and various internal and external ventures. For us to succeed, everyone must participate. I am committing 2 percent of our revenues for development in this year's budget. I expect your own personal commitment in return.

The process for growth is entirely different. It begins with management's vision of a market that can be grown, of the values that will grow it, and a definition of a mission that will add the growth values to the market.

The growth process has three parts. The first is provided by the men and women who will drive growth; the second by the engines that willprovide the organizations for growth; and the third by the strategies that will bring growth by maximizing current assets, logically extending them, penetrating related market opportunities, and participating in emergent growth technologies.

---

1. In order to grow, find a customer to grow.
2. Commodity businesses suffocate new business growth.
3. Business continuity is always safer than growth opportunity.
4. Preoccupation with the investment required for growth diminishes its return.
5. Logical extension of mature businesses is illogical.
6. Contingencies forgive commitment.
7. Commitment to growth means willingness to risk principal.
8. Maturity is the progressive erosion of competitive advantage.
9. Strategic planning rearranges the deck chairs.
10. Operating out of experience always gives the same answers.
11. It is rarely a question of whose product is better—it is more likely a question of whose market intelligence is worse.
12. Current market share overstates future competitive position.
13. Matrix organization excels in protecting managers from the responsibilities of growth.
14. When a business lays the cornerstone of a new headquarters building, it has become mature.

Figure 1.9. The Analects of Mack Hanan.

The three parts of the growth process are different from the parts and pieces of the traditional process of caretaker management. The men and women who run growth businesses, the growth drivers, must be entrepreneurs. Their engines must be custom tailored for growing, more free formed, more flexible, and faster acting than historic business units. Their strategies must be unique to growth; not the strategies of doing the same things better or harder or longer but doing new and unique things.

Because growth is a quantum jump in profit-making over maintenance management, growth strategy is incomparable with competitive strategy. It makes its own demands on management, resources, and organization. It operates in its own way, both internally and in the marketplace. It must be incomparable because its objective is incomparable: to turn over earnings at a minimal annual rate of 20 to 30 percent. At this rate, it is easy to see that growth is elusive, that it is extraordinary, and that it imposes discontinuous strategies on management.

It is also easy to see why a growth market is the *sine qua non* of growth: a market that is growing or growable. If it is growing now, its growth must be accelerated. If it is not growing but is growable, its growth must be begun. One way or other, there must be a growth market. Without it, no growth is possible.

The reason why this is so provides the secret to growth strategy. No business can grow itself. Therefore, no business can grow by itself. Only a market can grow a business because only a market has the money. The more a market is grown, the more money it has to do business with us. That is why the growth of customers is the supreme management commitment.

Growing customers is different from growing our own lines of business or growing our market shares or even growing the value of our shareholders—all traditional objectives. It has nothing to do with "achieving a sustained competitive excellence" or "manufacturing and marketing quality products and services." It has to do with one dedication and one dedication alone: growing customers who will, in turn, grow us (see Figure 1.9).

If we understand that, we hold in our hands the key to growth.

2
Growth Market

Without a growth market—a market that is growing because of us or is growable by us—we cannot grow. If our market is growing, we must accelerate its growth. If it is not growing, we must find a way to make it grow. If we cannot make our market grow or if we cannot accelerate a market that is already growing, we will have no growth ourselves. That is why a growth market must be the first part of management's growth vision.

A growth market answers the question, Who will grow us if we grow them? This acknowledges the central proposition of growth strategy that says we cannot grow ourselves. Someone else must grow us; someone who has money and who will invest that money with us so that we will grow him or her. People who can do this are our growth customers. For them, we will be their growth suppliers. Either we will grow each other or neither of us will grow.

Why will our customers grow us? They will buy from us because we can grow them best. Why will we select certain customers to grow? We will grow them because they can grow us best in return. For this reason, the choice of our growth market is the single most crucial aspect of management's growth vision. If it is wrong, everything else can be right and it will not matter. If it is right, many components of our strategy can be wrong and it will not matter either.

When management sounds the call to grow, what it means—what it must mean—is that it has discovered a growth market. There is a group of people out there, management is saying, who are growing their businesses. Or they have all the requirements for growth but need help. We can give them the help they need, either to initiate their growth or drive it faster. These people are called hospital administrators or supermarket chain managers or bankers or chemicals processors—it makes no difference. They constitute a growth market. They have cost problems we are uniquely equipped to reduce. Or they have revenue opportunities we can help them realize in the most cost-effective manner. As a result of our help, their profits can be significantly improved.

As a result of being able to improve their profits, they will be enhanced. Their functions will throw off less cost. Their sales will yield more profitable revenues. In return for these premium values, they will reward us with a premium price. While their investment with us will be at a premium rate, so will their return. In this way, both of us will grow.

Finding Partnerable Customers

Growth is not the result of finding customers we can vend to, customers who will buy from us in volume at competitive prices adulterated with deals and discounts. We are not in search of markets we can sell to. We are looking for customers with whom we can form growth partnerships, win-win relationships in which both of us grow. Otherwise, if we envision only buyers for our products, we will come up with only a commodity business whose margins will be dependent on competitive price and performance. This will turn out to be a no-growth or slow-growth market to which we will be an alternate vendor, not a growth partner, and in which the basis of the relationship will be win-lose instead of win-win.

It is imperative that, from the start, we position ourselves as growers rather than vendors, as profit suppliers rather than product suppliers, as growth experts rather than expert manufacturers or marketers, as a business whose foremost knowledge is the business operations of its customers and how to improve their profit contribution rather than its own operations and how to make them "excellent." It is especially imperative that we envision partnerable customers as our market to be grown.

What are partnerable customers? We can find them by identifying three major characteristics:

1. Customers must want to grow. They must want to improve their profits by reducing the expenses being consumed by their key cost centers or by increasing the revenues being generated by their key

markets for their key product lines. *This means that we must know our customers.*

2. Customers must be growable by us. They must have the kind of expenses in their cost centers that we are expert in reducing or the kind of markets in which we are expert at increasing sales. *This means that we must know the customers' businesses.*

3. Customers must be willing to grow us in return. They must have an understanding of return on investment as the basis for decision-making and must be comfortable with approving premium investments that will return even greater premium profits. *This means that we must know the financial basis of the customers' purchasing policies.*

Customers who meet these three conditions are prime partner material. We will not have to sell them on the need or desirability to grow. They will be self-motivated. We will not have to educate them on the location of the main pressure points in their businesses that can be the sources of growth. They will be self-aware. We will not have to make them conscious of the advantages that can accrue to their industry statures as a result of growth. They will be self-conscious.

Market Segmentation Made Easy

When we choose the market that will be the core of our vision, we have solved the riddle—and penetrated the mystique—of market segmentation. We have defined our growth segments. There are two of them, no more and no less. One we can call "the growings." These are customers we are already growing right now either actively, with profit improvement aforethought, or passively and unwittingly. We may not have proven it, but we know we are. The second segment we can call "the growables." These are customers we are not currently growing but whose problems and opportunities make them susceptible to being grown by us.

Within each of these two segments that compose our growth market are two subsegments. They are part and parcel of both segments. Subsegment 1 is growth by reduced costs. Subsegment 2 is growth by increased sales. Every growth customer will fit one subsegment or the other. Some will fit both. These will be our best partners because we have two handles on their growth.

The first classification—growing or growable—defines our customers. The second classification—reduced costs or increased sales—defines our entry point into each customer's growth opportunity. It also pinpoints the customer decision-makers with whom we will have to partner. They will be the managers of the customer's functions whose costs we will reduce or whose revenues we will increase.

All profit is good profit. Therefore, from the point of view of our growth partners, it should not matter which way we grow them. A dollar dropped to their bottom line as a result of reducing a cost is equal in every way to a dollar's worth of new profits from sales. It can also be a good deal more cost effective to generate. But the manner in which we grow our customers may make a great deal of difference to us.

Customers whose principal growth comes from cost reduction tend to be mature businesses whose market shares have reached their maximum and can be enlarged mainly by trading share points with their competitors. Their growth by cost reduction, while welcome, has its limits. Costs can eventually be reduced only so far. But even more important is the fact that true growth is sales growth. Sales revenues—that is, markets—are always the prime movers of growth for our customers just as they must be for us. It is therefore essential that we become expert in our customers' markets and not just in their operating processes. We must know their sources of revenues and how to enlarge them. We must know who their growing and growable customers are and how they can be grown even more. This, we will find, is our ultimate wellspring of growth—not simply our customers but our customers' customers.

Participating in Customer Sales Growth

Unless we can participate in the sales growth of our customers, we will never be able to play an important role as growers of their business. We will be cut off from our customers' markets, the sources of their own growth. We will be deprived of knowing where their future growth is going to come from, how sizable it is most likely to be, what products they are required to offer in order to play a major role in their markets' growth, and what products we should be planning to make as far in advance as possible in order to help them the most.

If we have the ability to improve our customers' productivity by reducing the number of work hours required by one of their processes, we cannot rest with reducing their costs. We must help them find profitable use for the hours of work time we have released. We must become developers of new business for them if we are going to help them grow.

If we have the ability to improve our customers' use of capital by reducing their inventories, we cannot rest with reducing their costs. We must help them find profitable use for the space we have rescued. We must become developers of new business for them if we are going to help them grow.

Whenever we have the ability to reduce our customers' costs, we must find profitable investments for the dollars we have released so that they can put the money to work to make more money—more money than the freed-up costs alone can amount to. The best investment we can recommend ought to be with us, plowing back the customers' new profits into additional business. In this way, we can repeat the profit improvement process. Each time we complete a cycle of investment, return, reinvestment of the return and additional return, we are providing capital to our customers. This capital, generated from their own internal operations, is the lowest-cost source of funds they can obtain. At each reinvestment stage, they are using the funds that have been returned from their previous investments. Each investment in new profits pays for the next one.

Endlessly repeated, this is the partnership cycle. We prime the pump by making the first infusion of new profits into our customers' businesses. They reward us with a premium investment. Then we ask them to reinvest with us. With each transaction, both we and our customer grow.

Within our market segments, we must achieve dominance. That is, we must become their dominant source of incremental new profits by improving the functions in their business in which we claim expertise. Their operations in which we are "process smart" must have a lessened cost contribution when we have dealt with them, applying our expertise and our product and service systems. Their markets in which we are "sales smart" must have a heightened revenue contribution when we have dealt with them. That is how we and our growth partners will know that our partnership is working.

It is worth remembering that while we are absorbed in segmenting our markets based on their ability to be grown by us, our markets are simultaneously segmenting us. Of all their suppliers, who can grow them best? Each of us is asking the same question. This is why growth partnering works. Unlike vending, in which buyer and supplier ask directly adversarial questions—"Where can I get lowest price? Where can I get highest price?"—partners have a common objective. It is a mutual commitment to grow the customer. By doing so, the partners guarantee that there will also be a source of wealth to grow its supplier.

3
Growth Values

To enhance our own profits, we must first enhance the profits of our market. We do this through the growth values we deliver. These values, the deliverables we identify as our benefits, are the second part of the growth vision. They answer the question, What do we bring to the party?

Growers bring incremental profits. Nothing else will grow a market. Nor will anything else position a business as a grower. The question, What do we bring to the party? must be translated in this way: How many dollars of incremental profits can we bring to the customers we have chosen to grow? This tells us three things about growth values. They are expressed in terms of dollars. They are quantified, not narrative. And they must be significant in the customer's perception if they are going to be acknowledged as values.

If we cannot quantify our growth values, we have not clearly envisioned our market. We are insufficiently knowledgeable of its business functions—its operations and processes whose contributions to profits we are going to commit ourselves to improve. If the values we come up with are perceived as insignificant or irrelevant by our growth customers, we will not have a growth business. Either our capabilities are insufficient to grow a customer's business, or we do not know enough to apply them in a growth manner. These are the two cutoff points in growth planning. This is why they must be dealt with early on, at the visionary stage. They foretell what kind of a business opportunity we can expect even before we go to market to confirm it.

Vendors of commodity products have a different problem. They need to ask only, "Will it sell?" To get a yes answer, they must be able to offer comparable or superior product performance at comparable or lower price. The values they offer are the features and benefits of product performance: what goes into it in manufacture and what will come out of it in operation.

Adding Values to Customer Operations

Features and benefits are product attributes. They are the sums of our costs. Improved profits, on the other hand, are customer attributes. They are the sums of reduced customer costs, from either operating or opportunity expenses.

Vendors sell the sum of their own costs. Growers sell the sum of the improvements they can make in customer costs. Vendor values are, at best, intermediate values. Their products and services must first be made productive by their customers before they can throw off dollar values. Growth values, because they are already in the form of dollars, can be put to work by customers as soon as they begin to flow. The time value of money makes them more valuable.

Growth values escape the vendor's need to improve productivity and then prove that it can be converted into improved profits. The vendor must work from the premise that there is always a direct relationship between productivity and improved profits. Increase the one and the other rises along with it. Practice proves that this is not necessarily so. Productivity improvements coming from product features and benefits may not be transformed into profit improvement even though they enable a business function to be performed faster, less wastefully, or with fewer workers. Not enough cost may be reduced. Not enough revenue production may be accelerated. The basic cost and revenue structure of a customer operation may remain unaffected or so little affected that it is as if nothing had been done to it at all.

If a vendor can speed up a customer's process, it may save labor. But saving 1 or 2 hours a day, or allowing the operation to be performed by one and two-thirds workers instead of two workers is meaningless unless the freed-up labor can be usefully reallocated. This is easier done with the release of whole people than fractions of workers or portions of hours or partial workspace.

The direct dollars that management can envision being sold to customers in the form of growth values can come from only two sources. Both of them are within the businesses of customers, not our own. That puts them outside our control but within our power to influence. One source is customer business functions that have costs that we can reduce.

The other source is customer markets that have sales potential that we can increase. If we are going to grow our customers, these are the areas of their businesses to which we must bring growth values: improved profits from lowered costs in the one case; improved profits from higher sales in the other.

The Three
Specifications of Value

In both cases, our growth values will have to meet three specifications. These are the criteria by which all profits are judged:

1. Can we meet or exceed the minimum amount of dollars that is regarded as significant by customers in answer to their questions of *how much?*

2. Can we meet or come in ahead of the maximum amount of patient time that is regarded as sufficient by customers in answer to their questions of *how soon?*

3. Can we meet or exceed the minimum level of assurance that is regarded as necessary by customers in answer to their questions of *how sure?*

Growth values rarely meet all three specifications. Incremental new profits that successfully meet or exceed the maximum amount may not be deliverable within the minimum amount of time. The larger they are, the longer they may take and the less certainty they may offer. Major profit improvement, short time frames, and a high degree of certainty are found to coexist more in fantasy than in the real world of growth. In some instances, large profits are required. Customers must therefore wait longer to be grown. But in the majority of growth situations, the most desirable combination is soonness and certainty. This coupling best serves the interests of time value, which allows smaller sums to be put to work quickly so that they can be grown, and dependability.

In the delivery of growth values, speed and sureness will almost always count more than volume. They are also more credible since they are naturally compatible. Several smaller infusions of new profits, delivered in quick succession, will generally be preferable to the promise of a bonanza. They are also more achievable. This is their crucial characteristic. Because customers must be able to depend on our ability to grow them and because they will immediately plan to invest any new profits we commit to bring them well in advance of their delivery, reliability must be our middle name.

A Process for Proving Growth

Values are valueless unless they can be counted on. Promises of improved profits cannot be put in the bank. Only real dollars, received on time, improve profits. This means that if we plan to enter the value business, we must supply ourselves with two capabilities at the outset. One is a process of coming up with growth values for our customers on a consistent basis so that we will not fall short. The second is a process for proving our growth values before a customer does business with us so that our values become the cause of doing business with us rather than the result.

Proving growth imposes two requirements on us. We must, first of all, be knowledgeable about how to add growth to the business functions of customer businesses that we have marked out as "our game." In order to demonstrate our knowledge, we must come equipped with norms based on our experience of the range of new profits that customers can expect from doing business with us. "Our norm for reducing cost in a forecasting function or an inventory function or an assembly function like yours," we must be able to say, "is between this figure, which is our low end result and this figure that represents our high end. Our norm for increasing sales revenues in a market like yours," we must be able to say, "is between this low end and this high end."

Our norms certify our credibility. They verify our expertise by demonstrating our track record, proving that we know how to improve customers' profits by applying our skills and systems to their operations. They serve as samples of our proficiency, allowing customers to get a foretaste of what we can do for them. If we buttress our norms with case history support, we further reinforce our credibility with third-party testimony.

We gain additional advantage as well. As keeper of the norms, we can position ourselves as the industry expert and our norms as the industry standard in the businesses of our customers. Who else knows more about what results can be expected? Who else holds the industry yardstick against which all others must be compared? When we are able to position ourselves adroitly, those who choose to compete against us will face a twin dilemma. If they cannot exceed our norms, they prove our primacy. If they claim to be able to exceed them, they may not be believed.

The second requirement we must accept is to create a proving mechanism that quantifies our ability to benefit each customer within our norms. This will be our primary sales tool. Its effect will be to say to customers, you have seen our norms; now you can see by how much your profits will be improved within their range. Generally, we will come out on one side or the other of the median point. If we fall below it, we and our customer have our challenge set out for us. If we come out ahead of it, we will both share in a bonus.

The mechanism we use to quantify our growth values is a Profit Improvement Proposal along the lines of the model shown in Chapter 7 in Figure 7.8. The proposal says, "this is what you will have added to your bottom line: these incremental profit dollars at this rate of return. If it looks good to you, here is the investment you must make with us to get it and here is how the costs and benefits of our proposal compare, item by item that they affect, with your current operation."

Our growth values are the proposal's end product. if they can be substantiated on paper, they can prove themselves before customers make the investment with us that we seek, before we install our systems and train their people to use them, and before they need to wait to determine the results. As growers, we start with the results. The proof is in the proposal. Installation, implementation, and application act to validate our growth values, not to prove them. As prudent investors, no customers should be asked to commit their funds without proof in advance of their rate of return. When we furnish proof, we provide two values. One is the money, the new profits. The other is the profits' assured delivery, making them useful at once and thereby multiplying their dollar value.

4
Growth Mission

A growth market and the grower's values for it come together in the growth mission. This is the growers' dedication: their commitment to the objective of their businesses. As such, it charters two of the most important components of growth. One is the market to be grown. The other is the grower's power to grow it.

The mission is the third part of management's growth vision. It falls into place naturally as a consequence of determining the first two elements of the vision—the *who* and the *what*. The mission states *why*: why we bring our values to the market we have selected to grow and why we should be regarded by it as their preferred grower. By stating our mission as the third step in our vision, we guarantee its market drive. We will know for certain who composes the market we are going to grow. At the same time, we underwrite the source of our power to deliver growth. It will not be our technology. Nor will it be our processes, our products, or our systems. It will be the profits we can make happen in a customer's business.

There are two types of mission. One is a no-growth or slow-growth mission. The other mission is for fast, significant growth. Businesses on a lesser mission commit themselves to an array of constituencies. They offer something to everybody: good citizenship to their communities, good products to their customers, good treatments to their employees, and good dividends to their shareholders. They define themselves as manufacturers and marketers. The values they offer are classified as quality products and services, striving for if not indeed achieving excellence. This is their preoccupation: excellence in their own products and processes. They are infatuated by it, absorbed by it, and made nearsighted by it. They forget that excellence, even if it could be achieved, would be unaffordable both to them and to their customers. As such, it would be unmarketable. But worst of all, it is unnecessary. All that is necessary to be the industry missionary for growth is to make customers more excellent—that is, to help them improve the degree to which they excel—in profitability.

Singling Out the Prime Constituency

Businesses whose mission is to grow fast do it another way. They single out their prime constituency as growth customers. Some may be customers who are already being grown. The rest will be customers who are growable. Each will receive the same offer: to have their profit further improved. This added value will be delivered by the grower's abilities in two areas. The first is to construct an optimal system of management expertise, information, products, and services. The second is to apply the system to each growth customer's business.

When these commitments are set forth in a mission statement—in this case, for a manufacturer who markets through industrial distributors—they read like this:

> We are in the business of growing selected industrial distributors who are (1) already being grown by us and (2) growable by us so that their profits are improved by the application of our systems of business management expertise, market and competitive information, products, and services.

A mission statement of this sort begins with the market to be grown— the *who*. It specifies the value it will add to it—the *what* in the form of improved profits. It also tells *why*—this is what we are in business to do. If we want to commit to doing it best, we can commit to maximizing our customer's profits rather than merely improving them. From the customer's perspective, however, most managers will agree that while maximum improvement is best, optimal improvement is acceptable any time in any amount. Some profits are better than others but there is no such thing as bad profits.

Celebrating Customer Yield

The fast-growth mission is customer driven, customer derived, and customer defined. It takes the point of view that unless customers can be grown, there will be no chance to grow the shareholders. It positions manufacturing and marketing as capabilities, not what a business does but how it does it. Quality products and services are sources of improved customer profits, not profits in themselves. To deliver them instead of the profits they may yield is to become a commodity supplier with no hope of the high margins that can accelerate growth. As far as fast growth is concerned, "quality" has only one definition. It is the richness of incremental profits that can be bestowed on customers by businesses that are busy growing them.

PART 2
The Growth Process

5
Growth Drivers

Growth is impossible without entrepreneur managers to initiate it and accelerate it. In many companies, the unavailability of managers with an entrepreneur's skill system is the foremost constraint on growth. Some organizations are completely devoid of them. No organization can have enough. Yet, where are they to come from?

Independent entrepreneurs—the real McCoys of fast growth—hardly ever "come in from the cold" to join corporations. Nor do they stay long when they do. Other companies' corporate entrepreneurs can never be hired away in sufficient numbers or with sufficient certainty at the most necessary times even if they exist. In acquiring entrepreneur management skills, the "buy" option is an unlikely one. Corporate entrepreneurs must be made and they must be manufactured in-house as the most important products that a growth-driven company can produce.

How can a recurrent resource of entrepreneur managers be home grown?

It is a growth truism that to build a high-profit business, first find an entrepreneur and build the business around him or her. That is good advice, with one alteration: *first build the entrepreneur and then build the business*. Corporate entrepreneurs, or "corporateurs," can be built with a curriculum consisting of seven strategies that will make profit-center managers more entrepreneurial on a consistent basis. The curriculum must come out of a top management dedication to create a growth climate—a corporate environment that will attract, hold, and reward high-producing managers. The climate must concentrate on growth as the principal business objective. It must admit innovative strategies in reward systems, in organization, and in operating practices. Finally, it must emphasize the teaching of entrepreneur management as the prime growth strategy. No company can be a growth company unless it operates as a university for its entrepreneur managers.

The profit-center entrepreneur system of management is the direct antithesis of matrix management. When growth is the transcendent objective, matrix does not work. Texas Instruments, along with an increasing number of other organizations, has pointed its finger squarely at its matrix management system for declining profits, delayed new product introductions that missed market windows, and the loss of its longtime no. 1 sales position in semiconductors to Motorola. The matrix, TI found, creates a cumbersome overlapping of operating and strategic managements. It is blamed for perpetuating the company's excessive technical orientation to the subjugation of marketing and fostering a planning culture that pushed all decisions into the board-room.

TI has redefined its basic profit center to encompass a complete business. Each manager controls the total resource package needed to run the business—people, capital, and facilities. The manager's responsibility is for the total making and marketing of all products produced by the center, a giant step closer to the position description of the corporate entrepreneur.

The Driver

Corporate entrepreneurs—"drivers"—must be management team builders, business builders, and market builders. Above all, they must be driven by profit. This means they must understand the value they deliver to a market and how to quantify it as the basis for a premium unit price. In this way, they can grow their customers' businesses as well as their own.

The principal objective of drivers is to partner with their customers in joint profit improvement. The customers must profit by receiving an enhanced return on the investment made in the drivers. The drivers must profit by receiving an enhanced investment from the customer—premium prices—whose values are based on the customers' returns.

Growing Drivers

Entrepreneurs are born, not made. Corporate entrepreneurs can be made: They can be grown in-house by training in seven strategies that teach them drive-type leadership and management:

1. Leadership strategies
   a. Policy-making
   b. Lean teaming
   c. Customer building

2. Management strategies
   a. Profit-making
   b. Brand-building
   c. Leveraging
   d. Market-dominating

These strategies have been derived from the day-to-day operations of independent fast-growing entrepreneurs, men and women who have been extraordinarily successful in starting up new growth businesses— sometimes with the proverbial $25. The strategies that have worked for them have been modified for implementation inside the corporate context to make them more compatible with the practices and policies of major companies.

Leadership Strategies

Corporate managers who would become more entrepreneurial must be taught to lead their businesses by means of making profit policy, growing lean entrepreneurial teams, and building the profits of their key-account customers. Leading their teams to grow their businesses and leading their customers to incremental growth are the two acid tests of corporateur leadership.

1. *Policy-making.*   The no. 1 job of an entrepreneurial manager is to make profit policy. Policy means the allocation of business assets for maximum appreciation. Policy-making is distinct from decision-making. Decisions are the implementation of policy. They are therefore the delegated business of the entrepreneur's team rather than of the individual entrepreneur.

Growth business managers must be taught to make policy through managing the rate of return on their business investment. Optimal policy is achieved when the rate of return can no longer be improved without adding to or subtracting from the investment base of the business. As a policy-maker, the fast-growth manager's job is essentially twofold. One is to drive the business from sales at high margins. The other is to keep down costs, especially overhead. Policy should be evaluated by the degree to which it optimizes profit commensurate with a minimal investment base.

2. *Lean teaming.* Entrepreneur managers make business policies. Their implementation is carried out through business teams, minimal groups of managers in the four disciplines of sales, technical, finance, and data. The teams, are committed to achieving the same policy objectives because they also share in the growth profits.

Growth business managers must be taught to grow the proficiency of their business teams by managing performance according to nontraditional standards. Shared participation must be assured along with shared rewards. Within the boundary layers set by the entrepreneur manager's policy, they must be encouraged to be acutely market sensitive, achievement oriented, and self-actualizing.

3. *Customer building.* The entrepreneurial approach to growing a business is to grow the key customers of the business. They, in turn, force growth back upon the entrepreneur. Businesses are built entrepreneurially not by building products or processes but by building customers. This is an entrepreneur manager's transcendent task, the *sine qua non* of growing a business fast.

Growth business managers must be taught how to apply the strategies of growth market segmentation, marketcentering, key account databasing and penetration, and Consultative Selling[1] to help build customer businesses. They enable a growth business to zero in on a customer's ultimate need, that of an enhanced bottom line, and benefit it by reducing customer costs and increasing customer sales revenues. This approach positions the entrepreneur business as a source of new profits for its customers. At the same time, customer businesses are properly positioned as the entrepreneur's source of funds.

Management Strategies

Corporate managers must also be taught the management of their business by profit objectives, the skills of product and service branding to achieve premium profits through premium unit price capability, the use of marketing rather than engineering for leverage, and the strategies of market dominance.

1. *Profit-making.* Entrepreneurs manage by a single objective, profit. They visualize their businesses as money machines instead of as product manufactories. Accordingly, their loyalty is not to products or markets or even strategies unless they prove conducive to maximum profits. Loyalty goes to profits and to profits alone.

[1]Consultative Selling is the registered trademark of Mack Hanan.

Growth business managers must be taught how to minimize the cost of optimizing profit on sales. The two indicators to keep their eyes on are their percentage profit on sales—which teaches them to grow profit and not simply sales volume—and their percent investment turnover—which teaches them to use sales as the drive-wheel to maximize capital circulation.

2. *Brand-building.* A growth business ends when its products become competitively depositioned as commodities—that is, when they are no longer capable of commanding premium unit price. At that point, future profit accumulation will depend on increased volume at decreased margins, the exact opposite strategy to growth.

Growth business managers must be taught how to brand their offerings so that they merit premium price by conferring a premium value on their users. In that way, price can be value based rather than cost based or competitor based. All entrepreneurial skills converge on the capability of premium pricing, for which branding is the principal contributor.

3. *Leveraging.* The leverage in an entrepreneurial business is in its marketing, not its technology. Only marketing can create the perception of premium value on which branding, and therefore premium pricing, depend. No matter how exotic the technology of a growth business may be, technical superiority alone is unmarketable unless it is converted to a premium user value by marketing.

Growth business managers must be taught how to use marketing as their leverage on profit-making by regarding their customers as investors and their sales offerings as investment proposals. They must also learn to avoid the two fatal dangers of overengineering their product and thereby overcosting it or underresearching their markets and thereby undervaluing them.

4. *Market-dominating.* A fast-growth business creates a transient monopoly. It temporarily preempts a market, becoming the standard performer of its industry. Two forces for change will end the monopoly. One is changing market needs. The other is competition whose offerings will break down branding. When premium value is lost, the right to premium price is lost with it.

Growth business managers must be taught to dominate their categories by adding incomparable value to their customers. It is always the customer who must be enhanced and less often the product. To make the product best while failing to teach the customer how to apply it best is to forsake dominance.

6
Growth Engines

Growth drivers must have growth engines to drive. Existing corporate organization forms lend themselves poorly to growth. They are too fat with overhead, too clogged with communication, and too tied to corporate culture. They move slowly, report excessively, and drag their asset bases with them like anchors. If the growth drivers are the jockeys, the growth engines are their horses. Both must be suited to the task.

There are ten basic models for growth engines plus two variations on them. Some models are designed to provide engines to maximize the growth of existing businesses. Other models are designed to enter new businesses. A few can go either way. The ten basic growth models, implemented singly or, more appropriately, in systems of two or more, comprise the compendium of new profitmaking engines:

1. Deglomerate
    a. Rejuvenated born-again profit center
    b. Maximize contribution from mature business—leverage past investment in asset base
    c. Minimal risk—growth within corporate culture
    d. Greenhouse for entrepreneur managers

2. Yeastbud
    a. Chartered task team—"bud" on existing operating division
    b. Extension of current technology
    c. Logical and sequential proliferation
    d. Semiautonomous yet controlled

3. Spinout
    a. Converted cost center into profit center

    b. Capitalize on market potential of internal service or support center

    c. Worst case achieve break-even

    d. Corporate subsidiary

4. Greenhouse
   a. Holding company for ventures
   b. In-house venture capitalist
   c. Grow businesses that can be brought into current divisions or become new divisions
   d. Joint venturer through minority investments and R&D partnerships or acquisitions

5. Joint venture
   a. New business created by mating two other businesses
   b. Equal control—equal equity
   c. Same or similar business as venturers
   d. Modernize technologies or penetrate new markets

6. Marketing partnership
   a. Market penetration strategy
   b. Shared risk and/or shared reward to finance and staff sales
   c. Systems capability without manufacturing
   d. Market presence without product

7. Development company
   a. Wholly owned subsidiary dedicated to diversification
   b. Bring new businesses into operating divisions or make into freestanding subsidiaries
   c. Joint ventures, minority investments, and acquisitions
   d. Act as darkroom for developing businesses

8. Skunk works
   a. Technology greenhouse with outhouse culture
   b. Quantum jump—break-through research
   c. Chartered science-based group to confront "challenge without constraint"
   d. Minimal supervision—maximum opportunity

9. R&D partnership
   a. Technology penetration strategy
   b. Shared risk and/or shared reward to finance and staff R&D
   c. Discovery capability without burden
   d. Leading edge without lag

10. Minority investment
    a. Invest in someone else's R&D
    b. Toehold in emergent growth technology
    c. Learn business without being in it—can buy out or bail out
    d. Multiple investments at under 20 percent each, hedge bets—keep options open

Some of the growth models in the compendium share common genetic traits:

1. A deglomerate is a born-again venture.
2. A spinout is a yeastbud that has been let go.
3. A development company is a spinout whose business is the development of other businesses.
4. A greenhouse is a development division instead of a development company. Like the yeastbud, it has not been let go.
5. A skunk works is a technology development spinout. It grows businesses from a science base while a development company is driven from a market base.
6. A minority investment funds someone else's venture. An R&D partnership is a stake in some else's skunk works.
7. A marketing partnership is a joint venture in cooperative marketing. An R&D partnership is a joint venture in cooperative science.

Each growth engine has an optimal role. Figure 6.1 shows the growth universe with its four concentric rings, each representing a different type of growth. One or more of the growth engines in the compendium is designed to fit the requirements of growth in each ring of the universe. If the existing asset base is to be grown, a deglomerate is the optimal growth engine. If base business capabilities are to be extended, a yeastbud or spinout will be optimal. To penetrate related market opportunities, a broad selection of growth engines is available: greenhouse, joint venture, marketing or R&D partnerships, development company, or skunk works. To participate in emergent growth technologies, the minority investment engine is optimal.

Growth Engines to Maximize Current Assets

Deglomerate

A deglomerate is a rejuvenated, born-again profit center. It is a device for leveraging a past investment in what has become a mature, slow-growth or no-growth business and maximizing the contribution from its asset base.

By pulling out a business unit from its department or division and deglomerizing it, a small fast-track organization can be created. It will have many of the attributes of a venture business. An entrepreneur manager can run it for accelerated growth. It can concentrate on serving a dedicated market with a concentrated product line. Yet it will rarely require new products. Current products, current markets, and the unit's existing sales force and distribution system are almost always sufficient.

Because familiar products and markets are still being managed by a deglomerate, it is a minimal-risk growth model. Substantial investment is unnecessary. Change is needed to instill an entrepreneur management style and growth strategies. Otherwise, growth can take place within the corporate culture. At the same time that a base business is being grown,

Figure 6.1. The growth universe.

a deglomerate can serve as a greenhouse for training and developing corporate entrepreneurs.

In Figure 6.2, the NCR Data Entry Systems Division is shown. Individual business units have been deglomerized from it, each with its own general manager, chief financial officer, R&D budget, manufacturing, personnel, and growth-incentive program.

Deglomerates recognize the role of small independent business units in generating growth. Business aggregation, whether in conglomerates of diverse businesses or agglomerates of similar businesses, tends to smother growth. It acts to shelter mature businesses in a comfortable environment, evaluating them by their contribution to cumulative division objectives rather than the maximization of their individual profit potential. Through deglomeration, a mature business can receive the concentration and dedication required to convert it into a growth business.

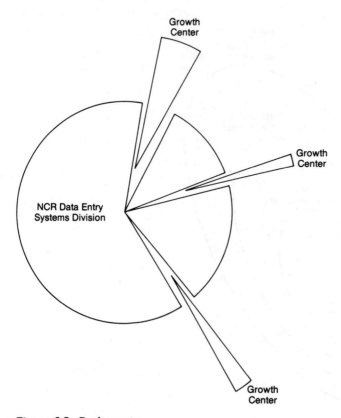

Figure 6.2. Deglomerate.

The upside potential of deglomerates varies. Significant new profits may come about from a small investment. Downside exposure is virtually nonexistent. The worst case is that nothing happens; the business is too far gone into maturity to be reborn. A deglomerized business may want to make partnership arrangements with external companies in the same or related technology or marketing, using the infusion of their capabilities to add new values to its offerings.

Growth Engines to Extend Base Business Capabilities

Yeastbud

A yeastbud is a hand's-length, not an arm's-length, growth business. Held closely by its parent department or division, it is set up as a bud on their organization structures. It has its own charter and works as a commissioned task team to extend a divisional technology, shape it into new product form, or penetrate a new market with it.

Yeastbuds are evolutionary extenders of current technology. If the extension is successful, a yeastbud can become a division of its own, or it can be reabsorbed into the division it has sprouted from. Otherwise, it will simply be cut off and spun out.

Through yeastbuds, a base business can be logically extended in a progressive low-risk manner. A series of yeastbuds can take sequential steps to extend a technology's reach. They can be created and disbanded at will. Since staffing is wholly internal, yeastbuds are culturally cohesive. People can come and go, moving to and from yeastbud and parent, without significant dislocation.

Yeastbuds are semiautonomous. They are always controlled, even though they may be geographically distant. In Figure 6.3, the IBM yeastbud that created the PC is shown. As an independent business unit, it was budded onto the Entry Systems Division located in Boca Raton, Florida, where it was far distant from IBM headquarters in Armonk, New York. The PC yeastbud's charter committed it to extending IBM computer capability into the microcomputer market within 18 months.

Yeastbuds can be given diverse missions with relatively small investment in workers and facilities. They can perform market analysis, arrange for product supply, act as assemblers rather than manufacturers, and organize new distribution channels. Figures 6.4 and 6.5 show how an automobile manufacturer like General Motors can extend its multiple technologies by yeastbudding. In Figure 6.4, flow technologies are used as a source of growth. Hydraulic technology, used in automobile transmissions and lubrication systems, can extend into new markets for liquid flow expertise. Similarly, carburetor technology can extend into new markets for air flow and mixture control while microchip technology can extend into new markets for electron flow.

In Figure 6.5, a second technology, propulsion, is shown being extended through yeastbuds. Piston propulsion used in cars and trucks, diesel propulsion used in locomotives, and small motor propulsion used in air conditioners and refrigerators can all serve to penetrate new growth markets.

Spinout

A spinout is an existing cost center that is spun out of its organization so that its cost can be unburdened and it can be converted into a profit center. Financial services, information services, communications services, and internal consulting services are logical candidates for spinout among typical corporate support centers. As going concerns, they may become profit contributors instead of cost-based services if other customers than their parent can be added to their constituencies.

Growth by spinout is progeneration, the development of growth business opportunity by capitalizing more fully on the market potential of existing service or support operations.

Because spun-out services tend to be mature, the worst case is that only break-even is achieved. The best case is that a spinout can become

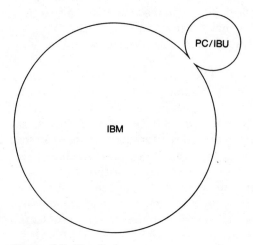

Figure 6.3. Yeastbud.

a freestanding subsidiary that contributes new profits. The technical expertise to become a profit-maker is already in place, resident in a service unit's expertise. Generally lacking are entrepreneur management and external market knowledge or marketing skill, all of which must be induced into a service before it is spun outside. Sometimes it is advisable to create a joint venture with an already-independent company in the same business, or merge with it, to speed the competitive acculturation process.

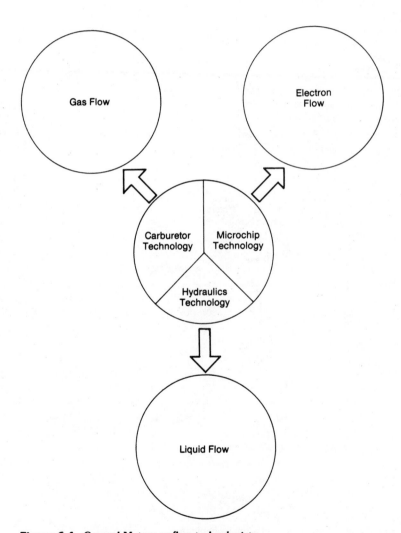

Figure 6.4. General Motors as flow technologists.

In Figure 6.6, the spinout of an internal consulting service from Control Data is shown, rechristened for its new mission of corporate subsidiary as CD Business Advisors Inc. Incorporation allows ownership shares to be distributed to its staff, providing an incentive to attract, motivate, and retain entrepreneur management. In this way, a spinout can grow entrepreneurs for itself and for its parent.

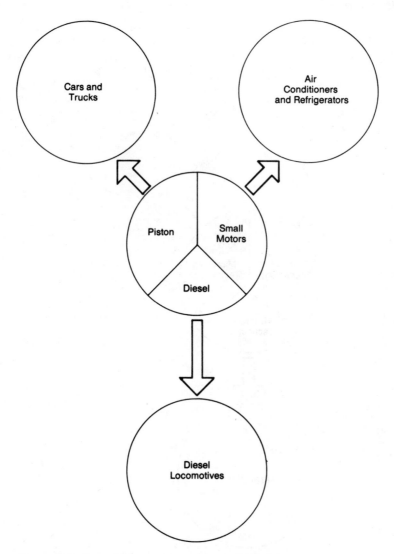

Figure 6.5. General Motors as propulsion technologists.

A parent and its spinout can be profit sources for each other. Profit, not organization proximity, must determine each engagement. The subsidiary must always have the right of refusal.

Figure 6.7 shows how an airline can extend its assets into growth businesses through spinout. As American Airlines has done, its training operations can become a school for other airline staffs; its maintenance functions can become fixed base operations for commercial, corporate, and private aircraft; and its telemarketing and leasing services can be used to conduct business for other customers and still serve the airline.

Each industry has its own specific spinout opportunities. A food processor can spin its purchasing organization into a commodities trading business that can profit from buying for several companies when economic conditions warrant rather than just for its parent's immediate needs. Railroads, banks, foresters, and extractive industries can spin out their land management services into real estate subsidiaries.

Growth Engines for Penetrating Related Market Opportunities

Greenhouse

A greenhouse is a holding company for internally developed business

Figure 6.6. Spinout.

ventures. It plays the role of in-house venture capitalist. As a corporate division itself, its mission is to develop business opportunities that can be new profit sources for other divisions or that can become divisions or subsidiaries.

Greenhousing seeks businesses that can penetrate related and preferably adjacent market opportunities that existing divisions would be unlikely to penetrate or for which they would not be adequate hosts.

In some companies, greenhouse management acts principally as an investor. Employees who develop product or business concepts may be funded with their own budgets to operate as start-up enterprises within the corporate context. Others may be provided with money, a line of credit, and spun out. In both types of venture, the parent company creates a partnership with its venturers. In the first case, it is an internal

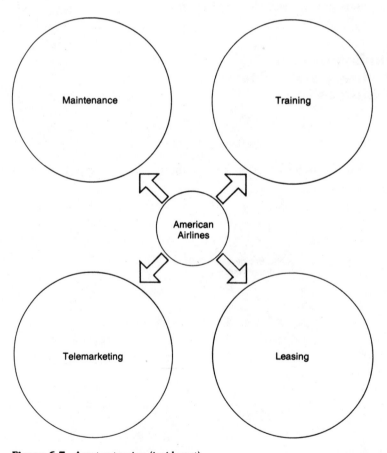

Figure 6.7. Asset extension (inside-out).

partnership. When a spinout is involved, the parent may receive equity in return for its investment and access to its equipment, facilities, and advice.

Figure 6.8 shows a greenhouse with four internal holdings. These ventures represent commitments by General Foods to penetrate new opportunities in its base market of women homemakers with its multiple base technologies. One venture, for example, drew from the freeze-dry technology of its pet food business to manufacture and market frozen skin-care products. Other stakes held by the General Foods greenhouse represented extensions of powder technology and flaking science.

A greenhouse may enhance its role by enabling its ventures to make toehold or foothold investments in freestanding businesses that can accelerate their probability of commercialization. These investments may range from minority representation to a marketing or R&D partnership and acquisition. The objective of joint venturing may be to offer a more comprehensive product or service, reduce development cost or risk, or to make an earlier market penetration.

The rank orders of these strategies may also be reversed. A greenhouse may first make an arrangement with an external venture, using its expertise and experience to seed an internal venture with technical or marketing ability. This can get its own venture off to a head start, reduce wheel spinning, assure entrepreneur management, and commence positive cash flow sooner, perhaps even immediately. Figure 6.9 shows

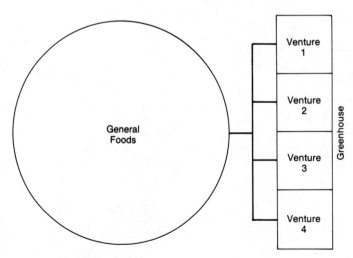

Figure 6.8. Greenhouse.

an enhanced greenhouse whose ventures are supplemented by acquisition and joint venture.

Joint Venture

A joint venture is a new business created by mating two or more other businesses. Each of the venturing businesses has equal investment and equal equity. The joint venture they form is a separate and individual entity, possessing its own management, mission, and capabilities.

Joint ventures are always in the same business as their venturers or are in a closely allied business. This reveals their purpose. The venturers have come together to combine capabilities and cultures so that a new business, enhanced by such a dual heritage, can produce what none of them could accomplish alone.

Each venturer contributes resources to the joint venture. Staff, process, and market knowledge are preeminent. One venturer may contribute advanced technology; it may have superior engineering or more cost-effective manufacturing skills. Another venturer may contribute advanced marketing; it may have superior market knowledge or marketing skills. Still another type of pairing may be based on complementary technologies, two differently based sciences that have a multiplier effect when joined or that can give the joint venture a quantum jump on competition.

Joint ventures may also be formed to modernize a mature technology,

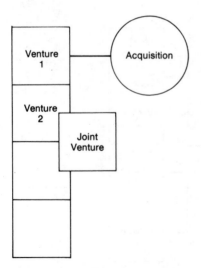

Figure 6.9. Enhanced greenhouse.

create a new and heretofore unknown technology, or combine efforts to produce a scientific breakthrough. Less frequently, joint ventures will be dedicated to penetrate a new or emergent market, such as the home information and entertainment market that combines show business, education, sports, and information and requires the joint capabilities of businesses in telecommunications, information processing, entertainment, insurance, or banking.

In Figure 6.10, a joint venture between General Motors and Toyota is shown to have created a new automobile manufacturer called New United Motor Manufacturing Inc. (NUMMI). The venture is designed to produce General Motors Chevrolet cars using Toyota automated manufacturing and Japanese labor-management methods. General Motors is also contributing its knowledge of the American car market and its nationwide distribution system.

A joint venture like NUMMI can become an immediate major player in its industry. It can renew the capabilities of the venturers as each learns from the other, enabling it by transfer to modernize its base technologies, diversify its product lines, and move into new markets.

Marketing Partnership

A marketing partnership is a sales extension. Its mission is to add to the sales capabilities of its partners by extending the comprehensiveness of a product line or extending its reach into an existing or new market.

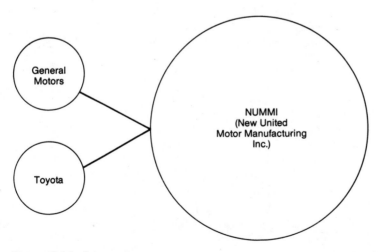

Figure 6.10. Joint venture.

From a make-or-buy perspective, it is a "buy" decision by both partners. For the line extended, the alternative would be self-manufacture. For the market extended, the alternative would be sales-force expansion, distribution, and advertising.

When a partner who has a product with small market penetration meets a partner with extensive market reach for whom the product is complementary to an established line, the basis for a marketing partnership exists. The costs to both partners are immediately reduced and speed of market penetration from the onset of new sales is increased. The line-extending partner can become a stronger competitor. This partner has an assured customer in the other partner just as that partner has an exclusively dedicated supplier in the line-extending partner.

In Figure 6.11, a marketing partnership between Iconix and Xerox is shown. Iconix makes computerized graphics systems that are sold to customer decision-makers who buy and use Xerox office systems. Xerox is enhanced by Iconix high-resolution graphics. Iconix contributes products to the partnerhsip. Xerox contributes its sales force, support services, and installed customer base.

Development Company

A development company (DEVCO) is a wholly owned subsidiary that is dedicated to diversifying its parent company. It may accomplish its mission through logical or illogical extension. Unlike the yeastbud and greenhouse, which grow businesses at only hand's length from their

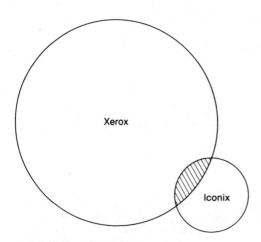

Figure 6.11. Marketing partnership.

parents, a development company operates at arm's length. It enjoys the conceptual freedom of being a separate company, the management freedom of being led by its own president, and, typically, a geographical freedom by being physically removed from parental headquarters.

Development companies are not in themselves growth businesses. They are searchers for growth businesses, analysts of them, and acquirers. They deal with opportune businesses as if they were venture capitalists. Some of these businesses they will being into their parents as new operating divisions. Others they will leave as freestanding subsidiaries. Still others will be subsumed into existing businesses.

Two common denominators mark most DEVCO operations. Businesses a DEVCO develops must represent superior growth opportunity, both in an absolute sense and in comparison with the parent's base business. They must also extend the base.

Figure 6.12 shows the R. J. Reynolds Development Company, a DEVCO to diversity its parent out of dependence on the cigarette business. The RJR DEVCO looks for high turnover consumables, disposables, and usables to complement its parent's expertise in mass manufacture, mass physical distribution, and mass advertising distribution.

DEVCO presidents report on a straight line to their parents' Board, where responsibility for the future is based. DEVCO staffs are business

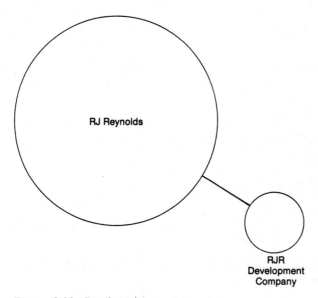

Figure 6.12. Development company.

analysts. They do not manage the businesses they develop. Nor does the DEVCO operate them, instead playing a consultant role and acting as financial agent in the disbursement of parent company funds that have been staked to the DEVCO.

Rather than starting from scratch as a cost center, an enhanced model of a DEVCO can house one or more existing businesses of the parent that can throw off cash to help fund its operations. In return, the DEVCO is expected to counsel these businesses in accelerated growth. Figure 6.13 shows the RJR DEVCO with two existing businesses in place.

Figure 6.14 shows how a DEVCO can approach growth logically. If a railroad is defined as a transportation system, a DEVCO can grow it by acquiring other rail lines and complementary freight shippers to create a "total transportation system." If, however, a railroad is defined in terms of its communications base as an information system, the movement of data over a fiberglass track parallel to the rail track is an illogical yet wholly complementary growth strategy.

Skunk Works

A skunk works is a technology greenhouse with an outhouse culture. A group of researchers and developers, preferably self-styled quantum jumpers, is remotely relocated "out back," left to their own devices

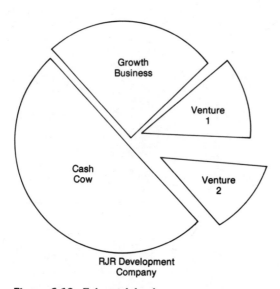

Figure 6.13. Enhanced development company.

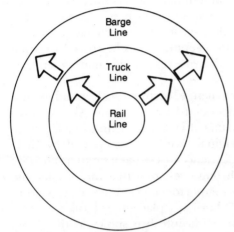

Railroad as Transportation System
(Freight Tracking and Transport)

Figure 6.14a. Logical extension.

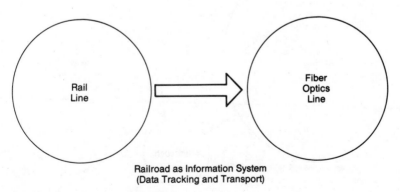

Railroad as Information System
(Data Tracking and Transport)

Figure 6.14b. Illogical extension.

under minimal supervision and widely spaced reporting schedules to achieve a technical break-through.

Skunk works reflect a corporate commitment to confront "challenge without constraint." In the belief that minimal supervision is conducive to maximum opportunity, a skunk works flourishes best in surroundings that are uncongenial to the parental sense of congeniality. Not only should the prying eyes of corporate Peeping Toms be forced to strain themselves to see what is going on. Their eyes should smart when they do.

Supplied with an appropriate challenge, fortified with a budget and incentives for achievement, and liberated from restraints, skunk works scientists are expected to be able to take their company into leading-edge businesses. Modeled after the original skunk works created by Kelly Johnson for Lockheed, an out-back science works has a singular mission: to dedicate itself to truly break-through research that can become the base for new lines of business offering performance supremacy. Neither pure science nor competitive R&D have any place in a skunk works.

In Figure 6.15, Apple Computer's Macintosh is shown as the skunk works in which it was invented. Even though Apple itself was a young entrepreneurial company, it was bureaucratically politicized. Break-through discovery that threatened the established product line would have otherwise been intolerable within the parent company's physical or cultural premises.

Skunk works directors must be scientist-entrepreneurs, invention-team builders as well as scientific leaders and business visionaries. Above

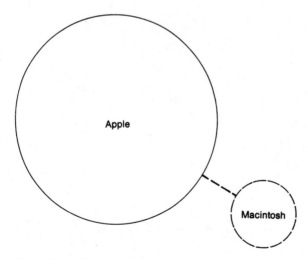

Figure 6.15. Skunk works.

all, they must be guided by the eventual business applications of their discoveries. Market values must be their transcendant specifications. Their teams should be small, topnotch, like-minded, and of the directors' choosing. Since break-through is such a high-risk objective, the team can be split into groups, each pursuing two or more parallel approaches. Each group will work toward the same objective but will work differently.

Quite apart from break-throughs, the fallout values from skunk works discoveries can have salubrious effects on existing products and processes, as well as suggest new products not previously planned or even anticipated.

R&D Partnership

An R&D partnership is a science laboratory. Its mission is to grow leading-edge technology that neither partner possesses individually or could develop independently. The contributing technologies may each be extensions of a partner's base science. But the result of the partnership should be a break-through.

In this regard, an R&D partnership is a joint skunk works whose costs, risks, and rewards will be shared by the partners. Each sponsor can maximize resources. As soon as a technology has been developed, the objectives of the partnership will be achieved. These may be summarized as creating an enhanced discovery capability without undue burden on the financial or talent resources of the partners, plus achieving a leading technological position without undue lag.

In Figure 6.16, an R&D partnership between General Motors and the Japanese company Fanuc is shown. The resulting organization, GMF Robotics Corporation, combines Fanuc's robotics technology with General Motors' automotive assembly line technology. Its objective is to accelerate the development of a completely automated factory.

Growth Engine for Participating in Emergent Growth Technologies

Minority Investment

A minority investment is a method for funding someone else's R&D in return for learning its technology, influencing its direction, securing a first option on its purchase or use, and being in a position to increase the

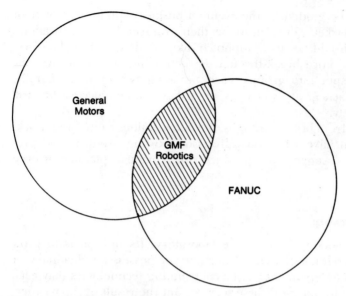

Figure 6.16. R&D partnership.

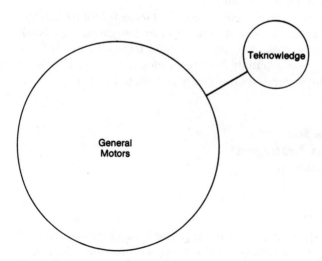

Figure 6.17. Minority investment.

minority stake to eventual total ownership. It is an ideal strategy for securing an early toehold in emergent growth technologies.

For a large company, minority investments are a form of external R&D. New business opportunities can be explored without initial start-up costs or full-scale commitment to enter them as an active player. Minority investments buy time. They buy a preferential place at the front of the line for emerging new sciences. And they buy the right to further buy in, to buy out, or to bail out.

Minority investments are generally at or below the 20 percent level of ownership. Not only does this help hedge bets and keep options open, it also permits multiple investments in several technologies as a way of evaluating competitive approaches while straddling a determination of the ultimate winner. Cross-buying in this way can permit investors to

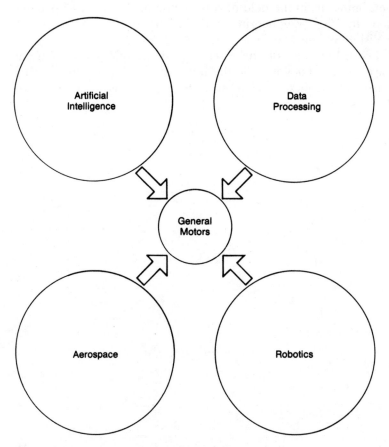

Figure 6.18. Asset acquisition (outside-in).

cross-fertilize their knowledge and create their own amalgam of the best attributes of several approaches.

Early minority investment buys a window on technology development. The investor has a catbird seat to learn how a new science must be managed, how its assets and liabilities match up, how it compares with competitive sciences, how it must be resourced both technologically and financially, what may be its most likely commercializations and when they can occur, and where the most optimal market opportunities may be found.

Figure 6.17 shows a minority investment made by General Motors in Teknowledge, a developer of artificial intelligence "expert systems" that can drive GM's automated assembly functions. General Motors has an initial 11 percent stake in Teknowledge along with a 15 percent investment in Applied Intelligent Systems, another artificial intelligence developer. Similarly, in the field of robotic vision, GM has a 15 percent investment in View Engineering and an 18 percent ownership of Robotic Vision Systems.

In Figure 6.18, some of the asset acquisition spin-ins of General Motors are shown. They include the minority investments in artificial intelligence and robotics as well as outright acquisitions in data processing and aerospace.

PART 3
The Growth Strategies

7

Growth Strategies for Maximization, Extension, and Penetration

Growth engines go nowhere without growth strategies. Traditional strategies go nowhere toward growth. Dedicated to small, steady incremental gain irrespective of—and sometimes to the detriment of—profit, slow-growth and no-growth strategies are incapable of significant maximization of existing asset bases, extension of base capabilities, or penetration of new market opportunity. For these objectives, only growth strategies will suffice.

There are nine basic model growth strategies. Eight strategies are designed for maximization, extension, and penetration. The ninth strategy is designed for growth by participation in emergent technology. The nine basic strategy models, implemented in systems combining most or all of them, comprise the compendium of new profitmaking strategies. The following is an outline of the eight strategies:

1. *Growth nicheing*
   a. Answering the question "Who can we grow?"
   b. Two-tier market segmentation
   c. Defining "our game"—our area of growth expertise

2. *Growth branding*
   a. The brand formula: premium value > premium price
   b. Ruling out debate on the merits
   c. Customer-driven pricing

3. *Growth valuing*
   a. Dealing in values, not products
   b. Creating customer-specific values
   c. Putting an "investment value" on the "applied value"

4. *Growth teaming*
   a. Entrepreneur model-building
   b. Teach-learn partnerships
   c. Joint growth planning

5. *Growth databasing*
   a. Key customer data systems
   b. Sales-data partnership
   c. Managing a growth database

6. *Growth marketcentering*
   a. Marketcentering criteria
   b. Business manager priorities
   c. Internal and external service contracts

7. *Growth consulting*
   a. Consultative Selling disciplines
   b. Cost-benefit analysis
   c. Key account penetration planning

8. *Growth partnering*
   a. Growth partnering models
   b. Managing, compensating, and organizing partnerships
   c. Partnership types and implications

Growth Nicheing

No-growth or slow-growth markets are mass markets. They represent maturity's endless search for volume—making up in quantity what is lost in unit margins. When there is no growth, every potential customer must be sought out and sold. No one must get away. A 90 percent share of market today demands a 91 percent share tomorrow. Most managers like to say they will not stop share-building until they have 100 percent of their market. Some, with a nod to the spirit of competition, settle for a mere 99 percent.

Broad, deep markets are costly markets. The Pareto principle tells us that 20 percent of all customers, often even less, can account for more than 80 percent of profits. These are core customers: the heavy profit contributors. They may or may not be high-volume customers. But they constitute the market as far as profits from sales are concerned.

The remaining 80 percent or so of all customers yields as little as 20 percent or less of all profits. Even worse, they are the source of a disproportionate amount of costs. They are costly to identify. They are costly to convert. They are costly to serve. They are costly to maintain. Yet being driven by volume leaves no choice. We must sell something to everybody. The need for incremental revenue outranks its incremental cost. The asset base must be recapitalized again and again. That requires cash and not necessarily profits. To obtain it, we must always improve productivity. Notably, we must sell harder.

Hodgepodging versus Eighty-Twentying

Volume markets are hodgepodges. They contain heavy users and light users mixed in with heavy profit contributors and light profit contributors. Many heavy users are light profit contributors because they buy on price. In contrast, there are light users who are heavy profit contributors because they buy on value. There are customers who could be divested without loss. Others who cost more to serve than they return could be divested at a gain. And there are customers whose loss would be irreparable because they are the basic source of profits.

Hodgepodge markets are an unaffordable liability. They, and the volume-based business that supplies them, must be down-sized for growth. Otherwise the costs of marketing volume—inventorying it, warehousing it, distributing it, selling it, collecting on it—will overwhelm the profits from marketing volume. Instead of "something for somebody" or "everything for somebody," growth depends on supplying "something to make somebody special." The concepts of "everything" and "everybody" must go. Growth is the result of progressive market narrowing.

Market narrowing begins with the 20 percent of customers who are currently contributing up to 80 percent of our profits from sales. These will be the core of our growth business. By definition, they assure it a high rate of per-unit profit. They have already discovered their ability to benefit significantly from doing business with us. In many cases, they have quantified our added value, compared it with our price, and classified us as a bargain—as a source of value that is greater than its cost. They are content to buy on the value they receive. Price loses its discriminatory role. Our margins are accepted.

Twenty-percent customers who pay premium margins are telling us something: We are growing them. The values we are adding to their profits, either by reducing their operating costs or increasing their sales revenues, are accelerating their growth. They are willing to pay us for the value of the new profits we are supplying. We may think of our transactions as "selling our product." Core customers know better. They think of us as improving their profits.

If customers are doing business with us to improve their profits, they will calculate the costs and benefits of their relationships with us. They will know the excess of their benefits over our cost. This will be their definition of margin. Unless we understand that this is how they buy, we will never know the true value of the benefits we provide. Our focus will be fixed on the investment we are making to generate the revenues we receive from them. These, however, are our own costs and benefits, not those of our customers. Ignorance of what we are really selling leads directly to our inability to price it fully. Poverty of customer knowledge insures poverty of supplier profits.

In order to grow, we must do everything we can to maintain a value-based price relationship with customers to whose growth we are already contributing. The only way to maintain it is to enhance it. This is our first priority. The second priority is to search out and serve additional customers we are not currently growing but whom we are equally able to grow. These will be our two growth markets. They are shown as the top of the market pyramid in Figure 7.1.

Committing ourselves to the two parts of our growth niche automatically dispels the myths and solves the mysteries of market segmentation. There are two segments of our narrowed market for growth. Currently grown customers are one. Growable customers are the other. Currently grown customers announce themselves readily by their willingness to pay growth margins. But growable customers whom we are not currently growing are obscure. We have not sought them out or we have not found the way to serve them. How can we induce them to come forward and declare themselves?

While we may not know who they are or where to find them, we already know one salient fact about them. Like our currently grown customers, our "growables" will have one or both of two needs we can fill. They have cost problems in functions of their business in which we have expertise in cost reduction. Or they have sales opportunities in markets of their business in which we have expertise in revenue improvement. Either attribute qualifies a business as a potential growth customer. Combined, both attributes qualify the business as a prime growth partner.

Growth begins with the market-narrowing question: *Who can we grow?* The answer will be the 20 percent of our customers who will, in turn, give us the growth that will make us competitive. They will be the customers who are right now paying unnecessary direct costs to run operations in their major business functions in which we are process smart. Or they will be the customers who are right now paying the unnecessary opportunity costs or unrealized sales in their major markets in which we are also process smart or sales smart. No others need apply.

Two-Tier Segmentation

Growing and growable customers make up a market whose narrowness seems exaggeratedly small when it is compared against a traditional mass market. Because it is profit based rather than volume based, it represents only 20 percent or so of the total market. Even though it accounts for up to 80 percent of profits, it may appear to be a fragile foundation for growth. What about the other 80 percent of the market—what should be done about it?

The 80-20 rule operates whether we recognize it or not. Every business is already deriving the majority of its profits from a minority of its customers. In most cases, though, there are no obvious signs that this is so. Heavy-volume users, not heavy-profit contributors, are worshipped. They get the special attention. Even if they are neither

Currently Growing Customers

Growable Customers

20% = 80%

80% = 20%

Slow-Growth/No-Growth Country

Figure 7.1. Growth country.

being grown nor are growable, they are given the same attention as customers who can be grown. This is because only their purchasing needs are sold to. Their needs for improved profits go unattended.

All profits are not created equal. Some profits are far more cost effectively earned, and therefore possess higher quality, than others. Nor are all customers equal in their ability to create profits for us. Only the top tier of our market will provide us with growth profits. This is why they will be our growth source. The bulk of the market, the bottom tier, will challenge our ability to sell to it in the most cost-effective manner. How low can we make our cost of sales? How effectively can we manage each customer relationship at that cost so that we maximize our earnings at minimal expenditure?

The Volume Trap

Volume is not the key to profits. High unit margins—premium prices—are the source of profits. Volume is their multiplier. A growth business has both. An increasing volume enhances the profit-making capability of high unit margins. At maturity, unit margins become depressed. Since the margins cannot be raised on each unit, the number of units must be raised if profits are to grow. As margins shrink further, the burden of ever-increasing volume becomes more and more oppressive. Volume offers salvation. It is also the profit trap.

Volume is not contrary to profits. But it is not directly proportional to them either. Unless our heavy-using customers pay full margins or buy at a premium price above them, they may be part of the 80 percent or more of all our customers that deliver only 20 percent or less of our profit. It may appear that "they are keeping us alive" because the cash flow pays the rent. Staying alive and growing, however, are two different things.

The 20 percent of customers who hold our growth in their hands are always our heavy-profit sources. Sometimes they are also our heavy-volume users. Far more often than not, the rank order of the profit-twenty will be different from the rank order of the volume-twenty. This tells something about growth. Volume customers typically support our commodity businesses. They help bring down our unit costs. They take advantage of it by bringing down our unit margins. Because they themselves are usually mature businesses, as testified by the size of the orders they place, they are highly price sensitive and cost constrained. Their growth is more likely to be accomplished by cost reduction than by sales revenue increases. They already control a sizeable market share that they cannot cost-effectively enlarge. Or they are in an oligopolistic industry in which sales revenues cannot be permanently gained but can only be traded back and forth among the oligarchs.

Growth is more predictably offered to us by smaller, faster-evolving business for whom market penetration and market share-building are urgent. They will be consistent purchasers. They will pay high margins because of the high value we can offer: the enhancement of their ability to sell at high margins. They, not the mature volume buyers, are our prime growables. They are already growing. Furthermore, they are dedicated to continue growth at a superior rate.

Our Game

The market of growables is the 20 percent market in which we are good at growing customers. It is the arena of our greatest expertise: it is our game. If we cannot grow at playing our game—doing what we are best at—we cannot grow at all.

Who we can grow is predetermined by what we are good at. But that puts the cart before the horse. If we are to be genuinely market driven, what we are good at should be predetermined by who we can grow. Narrowing the market to our most likely growth customers is the first step. It is the cause of growth.

If we are data processing systems suppliers, our game is improving customers' profits by applying data processing technology to some of their business functions. When we apply our technology to their inventory control and warehousing functions, we can reduce their costs. When we apply our technology to their credit and collection functions, we can increase their revenues. These are the ways in which we grow our customers. Our most growable customers will be businesses that depend heavily on the functions we can improve: multiproduct manufacturers will be our 20 percent.

Other than IBM, AT&T, and Japan Inc., all of whom are fully integrated suppliers, data processor manufacturers have had to find their own 20 percent niche:

Company	Niche
NCR	Retailing
Control Data	Science and engineering
Honeywell	Process control
Burroughs	Hospitals
Sperry	Government
Quantel	Professional football and basketball

If we are health care system suppliers, our game is improving customers' profits by applying health care technology to some of their business functions. When we apply our technology to their laboratory functions, we can reduce their costs. When we apply our technology to their staff training functions, we can increase their productivity. These are the ways in which we grow our customers. Our most growable customers will be businesses that depend heavily on the functions we can improve: large and medium hospitals and health maintenance organizations will be our 20 percent.

If we are building materials system suppliers, our game is improving customers' profits by applying building construction technology to some of their business functions. When we apply our technology to their materials handling functions, we can reduce their costs. When we apply our technology to their roof building functions, we can increase their revenues by accelerating the in-flow of rental income. These are the ways in which we grow our customers. Our most growable customers will be businesses that depend heavily on the functions we can improve: large commercial building contractors will be our 20 percent.

In each case, we have assumed two things. One is that we possess a dual capability for growing customers. We can grow them by reducing their costs. Or we can grow them by increasing their revenue-producing capacity. In reality, this may not always be true. We may be able to grow customers in only one of these two ways. The second assumption we have made is that our customers can be grown in both of these two ways. This may not always be true either.

Mature suppliers are the result of mature customers. If our customers are in a stable mode without growth or if they are in a negative growth mode, cost reduction will be paramount. Every cost advantage must be pursued. Unless we can help them increase their sales to their own growable customers, we may not be able to increase our own sales to them. We may be reduced to being partial growers. This is better than not growing them—and ourselves—at all. But to grow fully up to our capability, we will have to find customers whose sales revenues we can grow. These will be customers who are themselves growing because their customers are growing.

To a growing customer, sales revenues and market share, not cost reduction, are paramount. Customers we can help grow by further helping them increase profitable sales revenues are the *sine qua non* of growth. Without them, we can become only quasicompetitive. Our competitiveness will be limited by the same constraints that imprison our mature customers. They, and us along with them, will be constricted in growth by mature markets.

There may come a time when, in order to play our game, we may have to move away from our traditional customer base if it cannot be grown by increased sales to its own customers. We will have to seek out growth customers. These may be smaller, more entrepreneurial businesses than we are accustomed to serve. They will be on a growth curve whose demands can be different, in the frenzy of their pace and in their quality, from those we are accustomed to cope with. They may even be businesses in a different market—businesses with different cost structures and different customers of their own than our historic customerbase. Yet if we want to grow, we may be forced to re-niche our 20 percent market. The alternative is stark: for us and our mature markets to decline, decay, and divest in noncompetitive concert.

Growth Branding

Branding is the key to accelerated growth. Branded businesses and products are premium earners of growth profits becuase they and they alone can command premium price. The definition of a brand is based on this unique distinction: *a brand is a commander of premium price.* Growth businesses are businesses that have one or more price commanders in their mix.

Branding is not merely naming a product or trademarking it with the maker's signature or seal. That would be too easy. After all, many commodities are called by name. A brand, defined in capital-generating terms, is a product whose perceived value is noncompetitive. So superior is its perceived benefit that no competitive product or business can match its value in use.

It is an understatement to say that a brand's perceived premium value *justifies* a premium price. In reality, a brand's perceived premium value *requires* a premium price; or, said in another way, it *commands* price.

To equip a business to be a price commander, its products must be perceived by its market to offer unsurpassed value. The genesis of branding lies in this perception. To grow a business at an accelerated rate, it must be brought to branded status as quickly as possible and held there in command of premium price as long as possible. This guarantees its contribution of premium profits. Brand building has two basic rules: (1) Take off fast and high and (2) Stay high long.

Price command opens the door to profit leadership. It also permits the competitive isolation of a business. Rivals who try to erode the business's franchise by price cutting run the risk of reducing their own profit on sales. They also may underscore the price commander's superior perceived value by their contrast. In effect, they act unwittingly to validate the brand's claim to preemptive value. They tend to make commodities of each other, often leaving the price commander in sole possession of the market perception of preempted value.

The Brand Formula

A brand is a resolution of two forces. One is premium price. This is a brand's trademark. The other is premium value. This is a brand's "performance": what it does for its customers. These two variables must be in a specific relationship with each other for branding to occur. The customer must receive a premium value in order to justify a premium price. The price can be high, even ultrahigh. But the premium value must be perceived as being even higher.

Marketing is the principal branding function because it is the sole corporate mission with the capability of creating perceived value. True enough, value must be in the transaction before it can be perceived. But value is often present without ever being perceived. Conversely, genuinely superior value is not always present and yet a preemptive value of some sort is nonetheless perceived. How does preemptive value enter the perceptions of a market? In every case, marketing puts it there.

For a market, perceiving is believing. If a market perceives preemptive value in a product, the belief is that it is there. The converse is also true. Many premature commodities suffer from disbelief in their preemptive value. Many mature commodities can be rebranded if market belief in a regenerated preemptive value can be fostered.

The great majority of manufacturers excel in building physical value into their products. Few excel in marketing "use value." This is the primary constraint on the accelerated growth of most businesses. Their markets, like all markets, are expert in perceiving value. After all, that is what markets do all day. Yet manufacturers remain inexpert in marketing perceived value to them. This inequality of skill and the lack of common purpose between manufacturers and their markets account for a sizable number of new-product failures, short-lived brands, premature commodities, and mature commodities that fail to establish a branded repositioning.

Growth is completely dependent on premium profits. A growth strategy begins when we recognize that all profits initially reside in markets. Growing a business at an accelerated rate means capturing more of these profits faster. What kind of trade-off can we offer a market in return? The answer is always the same: a preemptive perceived value or, in business terms, a branded benefit.

When we develop new products, we act as spokespersons for the preemptive values that their markets must be able to perceive in them when they are commercialized. When we enlarge their market penetration, we act as translators of their preemptive value into the perceptions of the new market segments being penetrated. And when we turn around commodity products, we act as artificial inseminators of preemptive value into the perceptions of their traditional markets.

The value-to-price relationship of a brand may be expressed as follows: Premium value must always be perceived to be greater than premium price.

Perceived premium value (PPV) > Premium price (PP)

The premium value of a brand is its return. It is the brand's yield, the incremental net worth that it confers on its user. Because this return comes about as a result of the investment made to acquire it, a brand's price is not a cost but an investment. A cost is a price that does not bear a positive incremental return. An investment does.

The Concept of Perceived Value

When we define a brand's power as being derived from its *perceived value*, we are acknowledging the market genesis of branding. The perception of a product or a service as a brand originates in its market. While perceived value is sometimes directly correlated with manufactured or engineered value on a 1 to 1 basis, it often is not related to them. If we build a better mousetrap and that is all we do, it may not make any difference. Perceived value is based on value in use, not on value in the product. It is independent of the costs or technologies we put into a product. Perceived value is dependent only on the benefits that can be derived from the product.

The litmus test for perceived value is price. Markets pay for value. if high value is not perceived, a high price will not be paid. Price is therefore directly proportional to perceived value. The basis for premium price is what the market's perception of value will bear.

Growth strategy is the process of building high values into markets. There are times when this will require that added performance values be built into a product. There are other times when added values must be built into a product's sales or marketing approach while the physical product itself remains intact and unaffected. No matter what does or does not happen to the product, the marketing function must always add value if the perceptions of a market are to be engaged. This is the purpose of marketing: to create a perception of preemptive value.

Ruling Out Debate on the Merits

Debate on the relative merits of competitive products is the bane of business. Ingredients, components, construction features, performance standards and operating benefits; deals and discounts; service; and even a product's bells, whistles, and flags are routinely opened for buyer scrutiny in the hope that some marginal advantage that can justify the maintenance of price will be discerned. Products that are feature stripped and searched are, by definition, commodities. Brands are immune. How do brands rule out debate on the merits? The answer is straightforward: Brands are never marketed on the basis of their merits so they can never be compared according to them. Brands are marketed in line with the values they add to their users, not the values that have been added to their products.

The Lincoln-Cadillac case is an excellent example. For many years, Cadillac has outsold Lincoln by 6 or 7 to 1. Does this mean that Cadillac was 6 or 7 times technically superior? Automotive experts have said it was not. In fact, some of them have said that Lincoln was often the superior automobile in terms of construction and performance characteristics. How then did Cadillac outsell Lincoln? Lincoln's analysis is short and sweet. "Lincoln added superior value to its car. Cadillac adds superior value to the user."

So significant was this added user value that General Motors could say without effective challenge: "Cadillac is one of the few material possessions for which there is no true substitute." This reduced Lincoln to an untrue substitute or a true nonsubstitute for Cadillac. The validation of Cadillac's claim to brandedness was the inexorable criterion of return on the user's investment. Cadillac owners received greater trade-in value for their cars than Lincoln owners. Given the tangible superiority in resale dollars for a Cadillac, how much incentive was there for buyers of American-made fine cars to debate the merits of Cadillac construction and performance characteristics compared with Lincoln's? The return on investment said it all. It was the embodiment of superior perceived value.

Merits, which is another way of saying values added to a product, are for hagglers to debate in the commodity bazaar. Brands rise above debate.

Passing the Acid Test

There is an acid test for branding. It answers the question, are we branded or not? The test is singular and unfailing. We are branded if we are *the industry standard in delivering premier value to our customers.* The premium value we deliver cannot be a product or service. The premium value can only be growth: new profit dollars. This is the only value for which customers will consistently pay us a premium price. In turn, the premium price they pay us will be the basis of our own growth.

This is what "positioning" is all about. Either we are positioned as being branded or we are not positioned for growth. There is no other way to grow. Since no-growth or slow-growth is a recumbency and not an active posture, there is no other positioning.

To be positioned for growth, we must be positioned as the premier grower in our industry. Yet if we proclaim this position for ourselves, it will be self-serving and, therefore, self-defeating. Growers serve others, not themselves. Therefore, only the customers we grow can position us because they and they alone can testify credibly about our capability to grow them.

Branding is conferred on us by the customers we grow. This gives branding its authenticity. It also explains its rarity and why, like all things rare, it is so prized.

If we can become branded—that is, stamped with the imprint of a premier grower—we will hold in our hands the ultimate competitive weapon. Although our products and services may be equalized and their performance benefits reduced to parity by competitors, we need not lose our brand. Even worse, our products and services may be superseded, their performance benefits surpassed by competitors, and we can maintain our brand. We may be the high-cost supplier and the high-price supplier yet still maintain our position as the branded supplier. As long as we can confer premier growth, our customers will confer branding and premier profits back upon us.

This is the essence of the brand concept. It circumvents the chancey and transient nature of product or service superiority of the moment as the basis for profit-making. It says that product features and benefits are not the cause of branding; rather, it is the effect they can have on customer growth. It makes price not a function of cost or "fair market value"—in other words, competitive price—but of customer value: how much customer growth is worth. The customers pay us for the value of their growth. We now have the same incentive they have; namely, to make them grow. For the first time, we and our customers are partners and not adversaries.

Brand Pricing

The price of a brand has five characteristics:

1. Brand price is premium price.

2. Brand price is compared with the improved profit the brand contributes to a customer's business, not to competitive prices.

3. Brand price is recoverable by the customer's improved profit, eliminating price as a purchase decision.

4. Brand price is not negotiable.

5. Brand price varies in direct proportion to each customer's improved profit. This is the brand's "product." Since no two products are the same, no two prices can be the same.

These characteristics of brand price show how different it is from vendor pricing. This is because the effect of branding is to rule out price as the basis for purchase—the only basis that commodity selling has. Since a brand's purpose is to add value to its users—not to add a product to their inventories—brand price is attached to that value. It bears some proportion to its worth. The financial worth of the physical product or service that contributes to the customer's value is irrelevant. Its performance helps the customers achieve their added value. But it does not do so alone. Brand price does not reflect this partial contribution by being pinned to the product and nothing more. Instead, it is the consequence of the customer's total benefit.

Price is not the cause of customer value. It is the result. Commodity selling makes price the cause. It positions a low price as creating customer value by lowering acquisition cost. Brand pricing turns it around. The customer's value is the financial value added by the brander. This causes price, which is positioned as the result of the customer's incremental worth.

Branding makes pricing customer driven. It does not ask customers what price they would like to pay or if they think a certain price is fair. It asks what new value they need to receive and what investment they are willing to make to obtain it. Brand price gives evidence of what a benefit is worth to the customers who will be rewarded by it. It is not what we think it ought to be. It is what the customers think it is, based on their valuation of a dollar's worth to them at the point at which they do business with us.

By knowing how much value we stand for, we can measure our worth as an investment. We will know how good an option we are as a repository for our customers' discretionary funds. The higher our rate of return and the sooner it accrues, the better investment we will be. This is the "product" we will install in our customers' businesses, what we will put to work for them and what will improve their profits. When it is a good product—when its dollar-for-dollar performance is high—we can sell it with confidence and pride.

The value-basing of price forces us to know the value on which price will be based. Where can we look to find this value? It will always be in the life style or work style of our customers. We do not make value. Only our customers can make value. It comes out of the way they apply our products and services in their operations, their functions, and their processes. Value is performance value. It is value in use, not measurable at the point of manufacture or the point of sale but at the point of application and implementation.

Asking Brand Questions

The single most crucial component of brand strategy is determining a brand's value-based price point. It will almost always be higher than we first dare. This is because we are limited in our knowledge. We know a brand's cost. Only its users know its value and therefore what they will pay to gain it.

We can now see clearly the three questions of utmost significance that we must ask of each potential brand that we conceive:

1. *Who is its market?* That is, who will have value added to them?
2. *What value will they receive?* That is, how much added value will they benefit from?
3. *How much will it be worth to them?* That is, what will they invest to achieve the return?

The answer to the third question tells us the price. It comes from the answer to the second question, which tells us the basis for price. The area of knowledge represented by the second question is the brander's stock in trade. To know the value that we bring to our customers and not just the cost we represent is the database for brand price. To be a brander means to be a value-bringer. It is not enough to know we bring a value. Nor is it enough to know the nature of the value we bring. We must know *how much.*

Growth Valuing

Growth is based on customer enrichment. By enriching our customers, we differentiate them. We give them new wealth that enhances them and makes them stand out from their competitors. We make them "best." Or we give them new power than enables them to control their personal or business life styles, make them more productive and predictable, and allow them to reward others who depend on them. We brand them with the cachets of success, richness, and distinction.

In the process, we brand ourselves as different, too. We are no longer one of several alternate vendors, each with a parity product whose only true variation is price. We are growers. As such, we can tell branded customers when we see them. Someone is growing them by improving their profits. We can tell when we are branded too. We are being grown by our customers. They are paying us premium unit price.

There are, accordingly, two definitions of branding. The customers' definition says that branding is the profit difference between their business and the competition. The suppliers' definition says that branding is the ability to command premium price by conferring premium profit on customers. For both customers and their suppliers, branding is the same: *user differentiation.*

Branders deal in value, not products. To say the same thing in another way, brander's products are not physical tangible hardware but physical tangible profits for their customers. Branders sell money, new money that their customers would not have available to them without a brand partnership. Instead of asking, "How can we sell these customers?" branders ask, "How can we grow them, how can we add value to their businesses, and how can we improve their profits?"

Customer-Specific Values

Unlike vendors, each of whose products bear an off-the-shelf price, a brander's price originates with each customer. This means that there is no price that can be put on a brander's value until the value has been proved by a customer's business. Each value is customer specific. Branders, as a result, do not publish a price list. Nor do they sell products from a catalog.

On the shelf, a brander's products represent only costs. If these costs were simply to be transferred to customers in the form of price, the brander would become a commodity vendor. Instead, *branders create value.* Partly through the performance of their products, partly through the customer knowledge and applications expertise of their people, branders come into the businesses of their customers and create values that were not there before. When they have finished, their customers have greater worth.

There is no way to value branders exclusive of their performance. That is why proof of performance is so vital to branding, especially proof of a track record and proof in the form of a cost-benefit analysis that the track record can be applied to a specific customer's business. This accounts for the highly personal, individualistic relationship that each customer has with a brander.

Even though branders serve many customers in the same industry, they create individually different values for each of them. Customers who have never worked as partners with branders may ask them, "Will you do the same thing for my competitors?" If, by the same thing, the customer means will the branders improve competitor profits, the answer is yes. But the answer is no if the customer is asking if all competitors will have their profits improved by the same amount within the same time at the same degree of certainty. If that were to be the case, the brander would be a commodity vendor.

Branders leave their customers no choice but to value them on the values they create. These values come from branders' systems when they become operational within customers' businesses. Branders enter customers' manufacturing functions, for example, reduce the cost of processes and create new values. Or they enter customers' marketing functions, increase the sales revenues from markets and create new values. The new values that are created have been planned in advance. There are no surprises. Branders have based their prices on them. Customers have based their value-to-price relationship on them. They have already planned how to reinvest the new values. Some portion of the value they reinvest may be with the branders so that another cycle of profit improvement can be initiated. In such an event, customers are no longer playing with their own money. They are using incremental funds that branders have created for them—money that does not have to be drawn off from operating funds or reallocated from other priorities. This may be the greatest value that branders provide.

The Futility of Branding Product Values

The cycle of investment and reinvestment of the brander's values is unique to branding. It is impossible to accomplish with product values alone. This is why vendors must make every sale all over again as if it were the first sale. They lack inherent continuity because they cannot quantify the customer values, if any, that their products contribute. They pay in price for seeking to differentiate their products instead of their customers.

To the same extent that branders are obsessed with their customers and making them into winners, vendors are obsessed with their competitors and making them into losers. Branders try to enhance the objects of their obsession; vendors try to diminish them. In this regard, they enhance themselves, their products, and the processes by which they are made.

Secret or exclusive ingredients, magic formulas, and exotic formulations—"contented cows" from Borden's and the father-and-son assembly teams of Studebaker—are invoked by vendors to distinguish their parity products from all others. Continental Can's "econoweld" is American Can's "miraseam." Each welds tin-free steel cans seamlessly. Each adds value to the product. But what unique value is added to the customer? Unless there is an answer to this question, each will have to be sold on product value. Since both products have been equally valued, price will be equal too.

In the past half century, only two major products have been successfully branded on the basis of value that has been added to them. One was Xerox; the other was Polaroid. For approximately a generation, each commanded a brand price. But neither could prove a unique customer value to support a brand price when less expensive competition ended their honeymoons. They became commodities virtually overnight. Neither has ever recovered.

Because brand values are customer values, no one covets them more than customers themselves. In contrast, only vendors covet their product values. They explain them through infinite detail, exhibit them in close-up photomicrographs and cutaway drawings, and exalt them in purple prose. When they finish, customers ask, "How much?" When they reply, customers say, "Too much." The only way that customers can create added value is to reduce the vendor's added cost.

Putting a Value on the Value

No matter how much branders learn about the businesses of their customers, customers will know one thing that branders must discover anew with every transaction. Branders know how much value they can add. Only customers can put a value on the value; only customers can tell branders what their value will be worth. A brander can say, "I can improve your profits by $100,000." It is up to the customer to say, "That will be worth $250,000 to me in 18 months."

A customer will always set a value that is higher than a brander's face value. Branders deal in *applied value*. Customers take applied value and multiply it to its second derivative. They calculate its *invested value* based on what they plan to do with the applied value. They may invest it in their own businesses. Or they may invest it outside. Either way, they will use it for growth. The net worth of that growth will be the customer's concept of true value.

In business, value is used to beget value. Money makes money. Circulation of capital depends on the turnover principle for the velocity by which value is generated. The more money that can be circulated, the greater the multiplier effect of turnover can be. Branders affect both components of capital circulation. They inject new money into the customer's circulatory system. They also help the customer turn it over faster by providing premiere opportunities for its investment.

It is the customer's invested value—what it will amount to when it is calculated as "future value"—and not the brander's applied value that should be the basis of brand price.

Future value is the total value that will accrue by a given time as the result of a present investment. Time is therefore of the essence. The faster the brander can create values in customer businesses, the sooner that customers can invest them to make more. For this reason, because money exists only in time, there can be no consideration of dollar values without time values. Long time frames devalue money just as short time frames enrich its value. Branders' definitions of *what* they sell—money—are never complete, therefore, without their definition of *when* it will be available for use.

Vendors are constrained to deliver their product values on time. So are branders. For them, being on time involves more than having physical products on a customer's receiving dock. It means having new dollars in the customer's till. Nothing happens to make a customer more profitable by meeting a shipping date. That only transfers a cost from a supplier to a customer. Until a customer's business functions are affected—until a brander's appliers apply—value will remain to be seen.

Because branders' values are applications values, it is clear that branders are beholden to their application experts. They are entirely in their hands. They hold the brand posture. They control the effectiveness of the branders. If they are ineffective, the branders will become vendors.

When customers buy brands, they are really buying a brander's applications experts. These are the teams of consultative account representatives plus their technical, financial, and data support staffs. No brander can be better than they are. No matter how heavily capitalized a brander may be, branding is a labor-intensive business. Capital cannot apply itself; only people can apply. Capital cannot create partnerships with customer function managers; only people can partner. Capital—even in the form of product values—cannot brand; only people can create the customer values on which branding depends.

Forms of Enriched Value

The value that a brander can add to customers may take three forms. The most straightforward form is *improved profits*. They are always desirable, preferable by far to any other value by a profit-making business. They are advantageous for two other reasons as well. Profits are accurately measurable and immediately investable. They are the closest a customer can come to instant growth. This is equally true for branders as well, since their customers' profits—being measurable and investable—are immediately priceable.

A second form of customer value is *improved productivity*. It is specifically important to nonprofit and not-for-profit customers. Improved productivity provides incremental performance advantages. People and functions operate more cost-effectively. Either more output results from the same asset base or a smaller, reduced asset base yields the same output. Productivity is measurable, although not with the same exactitude as profits. But it cannot always be translated into a realizable value. Operating more cost effectively is an acceptable objective if growth is to be achieved through cost reduction. Growth through enlarged cash flow, however, depends on more than just elevated productivity. It depends on developing a demand base for the added capacity. Otherwise, productivity gains lead to unanswerable questions such as, "How do we utilize the one-third of a worker we've just freed up?"

A third value is *improved pride*. It is neither measurable nor investable. Nonetheless, it is demonstrable in such business attributes as heightened incentive, better morale, and even greater productivity. While feeling good and working well are not necessarily one and the same, feeling good may help reduce absenteeism, turnover, rejects, and callbacks. This, in turn, may have an improved effect on profits. Affecting pride alone is a brander's weakest position. But pride value is a worthwhile addition to profit value. In combination with productivity value, two unmeasurables do not add up to strength but their reinforcement effect on each other may accomplish what neither alone can do; brand a customer and merit a premium reward for the brander.

Maximizing the Value Market

Branders can add value to any business whose costs they can reduce or whose sales revenues they can increase by playing "our game"—applying their expertise and systems to customer operations when they are process smart and to customers' customers when they are market smart. Because brand growth is customer specific, some customers can be grown more than others. These are the customers whom the brander can enrich the most. They are also the same customers who have the greatest capability to enrich the brander. The scarcity of applications expertise, the absorbing demands imposed by partnering, and the time pressure to add values fast make it necessary for branders to concentrate. Where can they maximize their value-adding potential?

Within the brander's natural constituencies of growing and growable customers, brand strategy must vary with customer positioning. There are three basic positions in which branders will find their customers. Two of them compose the best market for value. They will help branders maximize their contributions and their resulting rewards.

Young entrepreneur companies that are in a fast-growth mode are one of the two categories of prime branding candidates. They can use all the added value they can get. The form in which it is most desirable to them will be added sales revenues, new sources of earnings that can further accelerate their market penetration and accumulation of market share. Growth businesses race the clock. They need to strike while the volume is hot, before competitors can mature them or an innovative technology can preempt them. They need money to manufacture, money to market, and money to expand. Because they are growing at a high rate, a brander can help them significantly even by only adding one or two percentage points to their growth.

The second category of prime candidates is well-established mature businesses that are in decline but are still growable. Unlike new growth companies for whom cost reduction is almost irrelevant as a growth strategy, mature businesses can be grown by reducing their costs as well as by increasing their market share. Since their asset base is already bought and paid for, and usually has underutilized capacity, incremental sales will add little incremental costs. They will be highly profitable. Any reduction in business function costs will further reduce the asset base burden, amplifying profits even more.

A large customer will have many businesses that can be grown or regrown. To the extent that they have the same business functions that the brander can affect, value can be added by cost reduction to multiple customers under the same roof. If some of them serve the same markets, the brander can help them add sales revenues as well.

A business in the third position, stability, is neither growing nor is it likely to be growable. It is therefore a noncandidate for branding. Stable businesses are static. They possess none of the dynamic instability of new growth or mature rejuvenation. New and mature businesses must grow. They have no alternative. If they cannot grow, a new business will become mature and mature businesses will become extinct. Stable businesses, on the other hand, must remain stable. If they were to destabilize themselves with an unreturnable investment or an unproductive—even worse, a counterproductive—market strategy, the loss would be unrecoverable. They would plunge into decline.

Instead of living in the hope of expansive growth, stable businesses live with the specter of decline. The chance to grow—to be branded—is not worth the risk of decline: Probable risk is greater than potential reward. Invitations to grow will be reacted to slowly, rationalized to a fare-the-well as to why they will not work—"Can it work here?"—and eventually rejected. Only when a stable business finally declines will it become a qualified candidate for branding.

Growth Teaming

Both internally and externally, growth is a shared process. No single function of a business can accomplish it alone. Two types of partnering must take place. Inside the business, two internal functions, profit-center management and sales management, must be teamed. Outside the business, they must partner with similar teams in the customer businesses that compose our niche market.

Internal teaming creates a new organization unit, the growth team. The team's objective is to drive growth. Its driver's mission is to grow the team's customer partners by reducing their cost problems and expanding their sales opportunities.

A model growth team and its customer counterpart are shown in Figures 7.2 and 7.3. They are the reciprocating machines that manufacture growth. The supplier team grows the customer team. The customer team grows the supplier team.

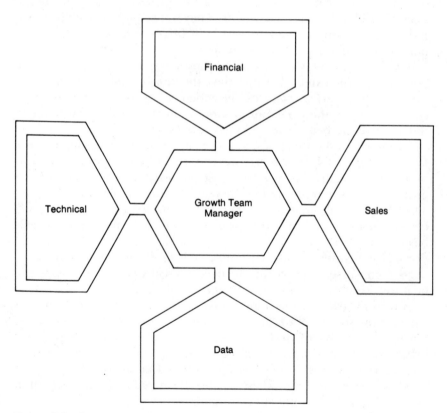

Figure 7.2. Growth team.

Each growth team is a microcosm of its total corporate power. Like a lens, it focuses the amorphous corporate strength on specific targets: a specific cost to be reduced by a specific amount in a specific customer business function or a specific amount of increased revenues to be gained by a specific customer line of business in a specific market segment. By combining internal capabilities that are ordinarily only loosely related and by concentrating them on selected objectives, growth becomes manageable. If there is a secret to business growth, it is in the one-to-one alliance of dedicated growth teams with their customer growth teams.

The Entrepreneur Capability

Because customers must be grown first before a business that supplies them can grow, the composition of a growth team is self-determining. A data manager is needed to validate where customers can be grown. A

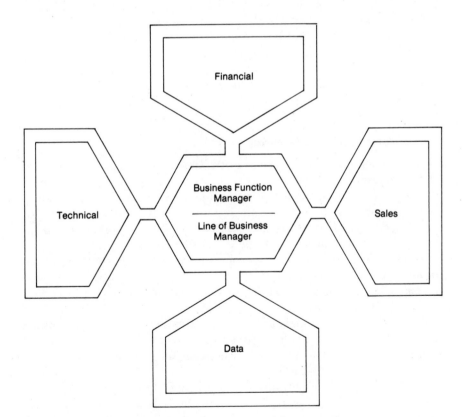

Figure 7.3. Customer growth team.

sales manager is needed to apply a product to customer operations so that it will grow their ability to profit. A financial manager is needed to quantify the amount and rate of new profit contribution. The driver coordinates the team and leads and manages them. This is the paramount responsibility. The driver selects the customers most likely to be growable. If the driver's selection is wrong, everything the team does can be right and yet no growth will result.

The ability to select a growth market—a market that is growing or that can be grown—is the quintessential entrepreneur capability.

Figure 7.2 shows the minimal team. All other resources can be drawn from the corporate asset base on a pro-tem basis as they are required, using the asset base for what it is—a mighty reservoir of talent and funds. External resources, usually of a specialized nature, can also be allied to the growth team when corporate staffs are neither adequate nor available.

Growth teams operate with simple charters. A team's objective is to grow one or more top-tier customers who will grow the team's profits in return. A team is evaluated by the customers it grows: how much growth it provides, at what rate, how dependably, and with what continuity. Since team growth is the reciprocal of customer growth, a growth team will be able to grow its own business in direct proportion to the rate, the amount, the dependability, and the continuity with which it grows its customers.

Entrepreneur Model-building

A growth team is a living laboratory. Its entrepreneur management style, its growth planning process, its customer partnering mode of doing business, and its profit-improvement strategies for consumating partnerships are a showcase for the organization as a whole. Managers of mature businesses can study the team's leadership, its organization, and operations. They can apply some or all of them selectively even to a business that is not yet ready to become newly competitive but is in a state of anticipation. This can give them a head start. Or it may provide the incentive for a manager who is on the fence to come forward and declare for competitive growth.

A living, working model also serves an additional purpose. A genuine growth manager is available on premises for counsel, providing internal consultation services to managers who want to grow and who need to find out firsthand what it is like.

In these ways, both by training and practice as well as by inspiration, growth teams build growers. The new profit dollars that growth represents are the immediate result of teaming growers. But the growers themselves, trained in entrepreneur management strategies and style, are the more enduring results.

Driver Standards of Performance

The driver's standards of performance are unique to the growth team. The driver performs five keystone strategies:

1. *Profit maximization.* The driver sets the dual profit objectives for the growth team. First the customer's profit improvement objectives are set, then the team's profit improvement objectives. This two-pronged emphasis on profit provides the team's entrepreneurial thrust. To implement it, the driver must pursue four additional strategies.

2. *Marketing leverage.* The driver must act as guardian of the product, making sure that it is left alone. Unless it is significantly deficient in the customers' perceptions, the driver must resist the temptation to renovate the product. Instead growth leverage must be managed through marketing strategies rather than technology.

3. *Minimal strategies.* The driver must keep the marketing strategy mix to a minimum, selecting the smallest number of strategies to apply against each growth customer that will insure the maximum improvement of customer profit. There are two compelling reasons to minimize the strategy mix. One is to permit cost-effectiveness by keeping the cost base down. The other is to permit the growth team to concentrate on applying a small system of strategies exceedingly well. Each strategy can then make its full contribution to customer growth.

4. *Product branding.* The driver must differentiate the offering from all others by supplying the most beneficial profit. The improved profit can be differentiated by its amount, its rate, or its dependability— or any combination. This brands the product. Branding gives the driver the right to command a premium price in return for premium value.

5. *Market dominance.* The driver must make the team's ability to improve customer profits the dominant source of growth in customer markets. The team must create the standards for customer growth. The profits that can be improved by customer cost reduction must become the customer-industry's standard cost reduction. Similarly, the profits that can be improved by customer revenue increases must become the customer-industry's standard revenue increase. Any rival teams who go up against the driver must fall short of these profit improvement standards in either their amount, their rate, or their dependability.

The drivers' roles may be summarized this way: they fulfill their standards of performance best when they keep the product from being renovated and the strategy mix from being enlarged beyond its minimum; at the same time, they leverage marketing to penetrate customer growth opportunity, brand their offerings to merit premium price, and position themselves and their teams as the dominant sources of profit supply for their industries. As a result, they are able to maximize the profits they contribute to their customers and to their companies.

Teach-Learn Partnerships

A growth team is a collective partnership among the driver and the team. They must share the twin objectives of growing their customers and thereby growing themselves. That is their shared responsibility. They must also share in the rewards. A team bonus based on incremental profits or a profit share is a common incentive. Since each member benefits only when the team as a whole benefits, the team can present a unified front to its customer correlates when it offers itself in partnership with them.

By itself, a growth team represents one half of a partnership. It needs a customer team in order to function. It must therefore take the initiative in teaching customers how to organize their teams and how to integrate them into a mutually beneficial partnership for profits. This is a team's initial sales challenge. It does not have to ask a customer to partner. Instead, it should teach the advantages of one-to-one growth teaming. When customers accept the invitation to organize growth teams of their own, they are implicitly accepting partnering.

The act of teaching the advantages of growth teaming is the first lesson in the growth curriculum. A growth team is essentially a teaching organization. It teaches customers how to improve their profits. Drawing on its general expertise in reducing the cost contribution of customer business functions and increasing the revenue contribution from customer markets, a growth team takes an educational position with its customers. "You are managing certain functions in an unnecessarily costly manner," the team says. "We have expertise in reducing these costs." Or the team will say, "You are unnecessarily underselling certain markets. We have expertise in raising these sales."

The growth team's function is to allow its customers to learn by doing. In order to conduct learning as partners, a customer's learning and doing must be in concert with the growth team. Both partners can then learn together. Customers learn profit improvement by working with growth teams to reduce their costs and increase their sales. At the same time, growth teams learn too. They learn about the customers' operations and how their peculiarities compare and contrast with industry norms. They learn about customer markets and what their needs are. Since costs can always be further reduced and sales revenues can always be increased, the partnership's work in teaching and learning will never be done.

A partnership can be said to begin when a customer perceives a supplier growth team as a source of its growth. This means that the team is no longer positioned as a supplier of products, services, or systems. It is no longer an alternate vendor. Its business is to supply improved profits on a partnered basis. The relationship between a growth team and its customers is not predicated on buying and selling commodity products on a price-performance basis. Instead, it is a financial relationship. The customer places premium investments with the team. This grows the team. The team transforms these investments into a premium rate of return that grows the customer.

Growth teams sell money, not products. They transact returns from investments, not sales. Their price is an investment, not a cost. Their performance is measured by the amount and rate of the customer's return, not product performance benefits. They work inside their customer businesses as partners, not from outside as vendors. They relate directly to customer business-function managers and profit-center managers, not purchasing agents. They work at these middle management levels on a long term, continuing basis, not from bid to bid. Their focus is not on competitive suppliers but on competitive profit-making for their customer partners and for themselves.

The best definition of growth teams characterizes them as customer growers. They go right to the source of growth, middle customer managers who control business function costs and center their company's profit-making responsibilities. They propose growth to these decision-makers, quantifying it in dollar terms of net profit and in percentage terms of rate of return on investment.

Both partners will become more proficient over time. Together, they will learn how each of them can earn greater growth profits by working together. This knowledge will reside in the heads of the members of the two growth teams. It will also be the stuff of which the team's joint database is made. The database will be the historical record of what happens when the growth team applies its expertise and its capabilties to the customer's business. This data will form the partnership's norms. It will also contain the priority rank ordering of as-yet unsolved customer problems and unrealized customer opportunities for future resolution.

Joint Growth Planning

Mature businesses plan alone. They plan in secret, in proprietary privacy lest competitors gain foreknowledge of this year's strategies for infringing on rival shares of market. If the truth were known, their competitors' plans are virtual replicas of their own. Except for the names, the plans of most mature businesses could be exchanged with each other without either adding to their competitive intelligence or altering very much about their strategies.

The bane of maturity is to plan against competition instead of planning, as growth businesses plan, to grow their customers. Mature plans are obsessed with their competitors' strengths and weaknesses. They itemize whose shares they will conquer and by how much. They stockpile contingencies against competitive strategies that have a low probability of taking place but a high threat value if ever they were activated. Meanwhile, the customer is segmented into product-based classifications but otherwise ignored.

When growth is the transcendant objective, planning alone becomes an anachronism. Since growth depends on customer growth, it is unthinkable to suppose that customers can be planned *for*. Customers can only be planned *with*. It is their growth that we must accelerate; their growth that we must integrate with; their shares of market that we must help expand; their competitors that we must help them anticipate and overcome. For these reasons, planning between growers must be joint.

The product of joint planning is a joint growth plan—mutual growth objectives and the strategy mix to achieve them that is prepared, implemented, and controlled in concert by the planners.

Each growth team has the same role in the joint planning process. It is to answer the question: *How can the customer partner best be grown?* The customer's growth team will set the plan's customer objectives. How much growth is required? How much growth must come from cost reduction—by what business functions? How much growth must come from increased sales revenues—from what lines of business sold to which markets?

At this point, the supplier growth team can go to work. Here is the contribution we can make to cost reduction—here are the business functions we can affect, here are the costs we can decrease, here are the profits we can save. Here is the contribution we can make to increased sales revenues—here are the markets we can affect, here are the lines of business whose sales we can increase, here are the profits we can add.

For the year as a whole, here are the new profit dollars you can expect from our growth partnership over the next 12 months. Is this a significant contribution? If not, what will be?

The plan that emerges is not "our plan" or "their plan" but a joint plan, a commitment to work together to achieve mutual profit improvement. Each major infusion of profits into the customer's business will come from a Profit Improvement Proposal.[1] Each proposal will improve profits by reducing a specific business function cost or increasing a line of business earnings from a specific customer market.

It is obvious that the act of implementing a jointly prepared plan can unite the partners who install it. Less obvious but equally binding, the act of preparing a joint plan can partner the growth teams as coconspirators in mutual profit enhancement. Would-be "third partners" have no operating base because they have no planning base. They can still sell as vendors. But the high margin, big winner sales will already have been planned for.

Growth Databasing

High margin profits are the essence of earnings growth. High margins depend on branding—the ability to command premium price. In turn, premium price capability is the result of delivering premium value to customers. Premium value is value that justifies a premium price.

How can premium price capability be obtained? There are three strategies that must be followed:

1. Customer accounts must be categorized according to two character-istics: the dollar values of their problems that we can solve and the corresponding dollar values of our solutions.

2. Customers must be penetrated at the highest relevant management level at which their problems can be most profitably solved.

3. Solutions must be presented in terms of new dollar values for our customers that can then become the basis for our premium price.

Each of these strategies is data dependent. Without accurate customer knowledge, the dollar values of customer problems, the dollar values of our solutions and the value-to-price leverage they afford us, and the entry points at which customer problems are most profitable to solve, will all be largely unknown. Sales strategy will then be forced back to the commodity approach of selling price-performance values at the pur-chasing agent entry level.

A key-account customer database is the central resource for high-margin branded selling. It contains within it the two crucial targets for profit-improvement selling: the amount of a customer's costs that we can help reduce or eliminate and the amount of new sales revenues we can help achieve. Without this knowledge, the transcendant admonition to "know the customer's business" has no meaning.

In the early 1970s, Cincinnati Milacron tried to market an early

---

[1]Profit Improvement Proposal is the registered trademark of the partnership selling process invented by Mack Hanan.

flexible manufacturing system, a novel grouping of several production machines under computer control. It failed. Milacron still thinks it got burned for being "too innovative." In reality, it asked the wrong question: "What is the most technically advanced equipment we can come up with?" Ten years later Milacron tried again, this time asking a question that brought the market in: "What will our customers feel most comfortable with?"

In retrospect, Milacron's original problem is clear. It was not an excess of innovation. It was a scarcity of knowledge about their customer businesses.

To sell at growth margins, customers' businesses must be perceived the way they themselves perceive them. Businesses are collections of costs. Some of these costs are direct. Dollar by dollar, they can watch them erode their profits. Every dollar of cost they can eliminate means more profit that can be dropped to the bottom line. Other costs are less direct. They are opportunity costs—the price they are paying for unrealized sales opportunities that could bring additional profits to the bottom line. These two areas of cost form the data platform of their businesses.

To use our sales function as a growth strategy, we will have to replicate the customers' data platforms. By doing so, we will internalize the customers: we bring their businesses into our business. Then we must add our database to theirs by matching our optimal solutions with their problems. In this way, our businesses can be merged in problem-solving partnerships. The customers' improved profits and our improved profits become the partnerships' common   bonds.

The Key Customer Data System

Key-account sales managers and their representatives must have customer growth as their primary mission. For customers in high-velocity markets, growth is the only mission. Many managers and representatives operate from a databased key account penetration system that is known by the acronym APACHE[2] (Accelerated Penetration at Customer High-Level Entry). An APACHE system is structured with five components:

1. Penetration objectives for earnings, revenues, and sales

2. Profit improvement strategies for key problems and opportunities

3. Profit improvement proposals for presentation

---

[2]APACHE is the registered trademark of the key account penetration and proposal system invented by Mack Hanan.

4. Penetration review strategies for account control

5. Penetration database

Every APACHE data system is organized on a key industry basis—the 20 percent or so of all customer industries that account for up to 80 percent of a company's profitable sales volume. The foundation of an APACHE system is always industry data. This includes information about the industry's life cycle that tells where it is in its growth curve, the industry's key ratios, its chief competitive factors, and the impact of the economic cycle on industry prosperity.

For a Marketcentered sales force that is dedicated to a single industry, this level of the APACHE data system will be its basing point. If a sales group serves multiple industries, it will work from several databases that are organized on an industry-by-industry basis.

Under the horizontal umbrella of each industry's information, the APACHE data system gets down to the increasingly vertical knowledge required to penetrate a customer and produce a sales proposal. There are six progressive levels of knowledge in an APACHE system:

1. *Key customer accounts.* On a key-account-by-key-account basis, each major actual and potential customer is profiled according to the current business mode of its life cycle, its key ratios and how they compare with the average ratios of its industry, and its divisional lines of business and their contributions and competitive positions.

2. *Key operating divisions.* Within each major account, each division that is an actual or potential key customer is profiled according to its current life cycle business mode, its key ratios and how they compare with competitors, its past and expected contribution to customer profit, sales objectives and costs, and the competitive positions of its main product lines.

3. *Key lines of business.* Within each division, each business line that is an actual or potential key customer is profiled according to its current life cycle business mode, its contribution to division profit, sales objectives and costs, and competitive position.

4. *Key business functions.* Within each line of business, each business function that is an actual or potential key customer is profiled according to its positive or negative contribution to business line profit, sales objectives, and costs. Its key management decision makers and their influencers can also be profiled.

5. *Key problems and opportunities.* Within each business function, the key customer problems that we can help solve and the key opportunities that we can help a customer seize are profiled according to the

dollar values of their present contribution to direct or opportunity costs. Each problem or opportunity must be solvable by us, profitable for us and a customer to solve, and our solution must be quantifiable in terms of improved customer profit.

6. *Key profit improvement solutions.* Each key problem or opportunity will be profiled in relation to our optimal solution. In some cases, a range of solutions will be indicated. Each solution will be defined according to our system of products and services that physically compose it and the incremental profit and rate of return on investment each system can contribute to each customer. The optimal solution will be proposed.

The Salesman-APACHE Partnership

An APACHE data system is a stockpile of key-account customer cost problems and sales revenue opportunities. It is, in effect, our growth market opportunity. APACHE is the ideal major customer support system. Our key-account sales managers and their representatives—who, after all, hold our most profitable sales opportunities in their hands—are the prime APACHE users. It is from APACHE data that they will create and sell the profit-improvement proposals whose premium prices will accelerate our own growth profits.

APACHE acts as our key account representatives' proposal partner. Our representatives can commune with their APACHE databases in the following manner:

"Tell me what you know about the power tool industry.

"What are the industry's growth trends and their projections? How does it stack up competitively? How is it being affected by the current economic cycle? Let me see Black & Decker's position in the industry. How do their trends and ratios compare to the industry and to their competitors?

"Give me a closer look at Black & Decker's power tools division. What are the major lines of business for its 6000 products? Which ones are the 20 percent that generate 80 percent or so of profitable sales volume? Now that I know their main sources of profit, where are the major cost centers?

"Give me the rank order of the power tool division's cost centers for hand-held tools arranged by business function. After that, give me the rank order of the division's sales opportunities for hand-held tools. I see some cost centers and sales opportunities that I may be able to attack in a combined manner.

tion of paint, glass, and ceramic products has been organized into a home Marketcenter.

Key Centering Criteria

In order for an organization to be truly Marketcentered, it must pass two acid tests: Is a market the focal point of its operations? Is the prime objective of the business to become the market's preferred central source for improving its profit? If the answers are yes to both tests, the business will most likely meet five key criteria:

1. *Need-based market definition.* The center will be chartered to serve a market that has been defined according to how we can help improve its profit. This permits the market to be served by a diversified system of products and services that, taken together, supply a combination of closely related benefits. We may market two or more related-use products in a single sale or package several products and their related services into a single unit.

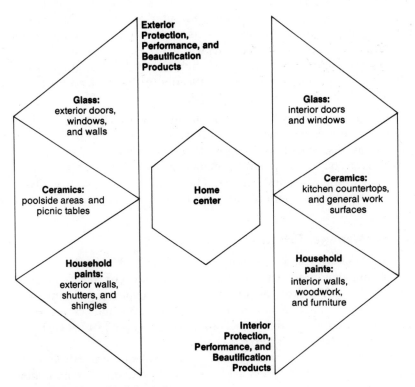

Figure 7.5. Home Marketcenter.

2. *Entrepreneur management.*   A Marketcenter is a profit center. To maximize its ability to contribute profit, its management style and practice must be entrepreneurial. Its chief executive officer will be a business manager who is fully responsible for profit. The entrepreneur should enjoy considerable authority in running the business, including price setting, cost control, and product and market management.

3. *Contractual support services.*   The business manager is the center's chief line manager. All other functions are repositioned to revolve about the manager in a satellite corporate support system. Business managers view their support systems as a menu. They pick and choose the precise type and amount of each corporate service they need for each mission and then engage the services they want on a contractual basis. They retain the right to refuse to do business with any internal service that cannot be competitive in price or performance benefits. In such cases, they can enter into contracts with external sources of supply.

4. *Database core.*   A Marketcenter brings its customers into the business by creating a market database that acts as its information center. The database contains their needs in computerized form. The center's storehouse of market information is its core asset, the source of its decision-making support. Its contents will feature two principal categories of knowledge: a quantification of the dollar values assigned by the market to its major needs and a quantification of the dollar values that the center can deliver to benefit each need.

5. *Top management role.*   A Marketcenter is a corporate holding. The role of top management is to act as a holding company for its centers or, as it is sometimes thought of, as a central bank. The bankers perform as a council of portfolio managers who fund the corporate investments in their business centers. They dispense consultative advice along with their money and are also available as a review board.

Business Manager Priorities

A business manager may head up a single large Marketcenter or a couple of smaller interrelated centers. In either event, the manager's priority is to maximize the rate of return on the corporate investment in a center. A minimum pretax return—say 25 percent—may be set as the manager's mandate, or a minimum range for increased annual earnings may be set at the 10 to 15 percent level.

Profit-center business managers have Marketcenter growth as their primary mission. For businesses that are centered on emerging new markets, growth is the only mission. Many managers operate from a databased profit-center planning system that is known by the acronym AZTEC[3] (Accelerated Ztrategies and Tactics for Entrepreneur Command). An AZTEC plan is structured with five components:

1. Branded business position plan
2. Growth objectives for earnings, revenues, and sales
3. Growth strategies for products, promotion, and pricing
4. Controls for growth evaluation and monitoring
5. Growth database

AZTEC contains no assumptions. There are no contingencies either since contingencies are the illegitmate children of assumptions. The unity of an AZTEC profit-center plan permits concentration on a single set of strategies. There is obvious pressure for them to be optimal. When unplannable factors occur, an AZTEC plan can be quickly restructured to take them into consideration.

As a correlate of the manager's concentration on financial bogeys, a Marketcenter's business manager tends to view profit creation as the position's prior commitment. It takes precedence over the stewardship of specific products or processes as well as the temptation to become addicted to a particular line of business or technology.

Money management is the business manager's primary role. The principal responsibility to operate the Marketcenter as a money machine requires the manager to focus on two targets. One is the market database. It must be nurtured with fresh information that is input on an as-received basis, coordinated with existing information, and made accessible in the full range of cross-references to which the manager and the company's staff support services refer. The care and feeding of the center's database is a business manager's overriding operational task.

Next in importance for the business manager is optimizing the use of the corporate and external support resources. They orbit around the manager's central position in a solar system of service options. This relationship is shown in Figure 7.6. There are four basic services that must be managed: development, production, promotion, and control.

1. Development services combine market research and development with new product R&D under a single director. In this way, the market orientation of R&D—historically one of the chief stumbling blocks to

---

[3]AZTEC is the registered trademark of the profit center planning system invented by Mack Hanan.

raising the corporate consciousness of customer needs—is accomplished organizationally. New market values, new process technology, and new product development are able to interact harmoniously rather than competitively. With Marketcentering, the traditional vice presidential functions for marketing and R&D can be subsumed under the director of development. There is generally no rationale for a vice president of marketing in such an organization. The entire corporate structure is market driven. In addition, business managers act as their own chief marketing officers.

2. Production services coordinate product engineering and manufacturing operations.

3. Promotion services combine sales, advertising, and publicity.

4. Control services perform the basic research to evaluate product marketing. They also provide the necessary recruitment, compensation, training and development, legal, and financial functions for the Marketcenter.

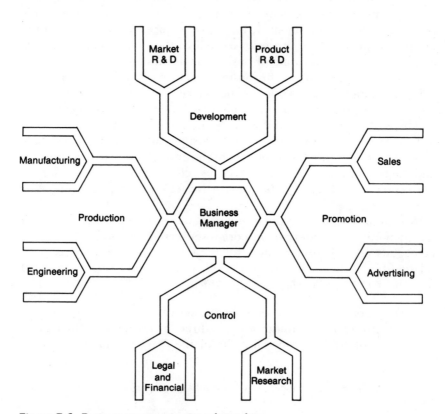

Figure 7.6. Business manager-service relationships.

Internal and External Service Contracts

A business manager may contract to retain one or all four internal services, either in whole or in part. The manager may also employ external services to supplement, complement, or take the place of internal services. The manager's ultimate responsibility for profit requires the freedom to negotiate with any operating service that meets product and market specifictions most cost effectively.

Much of the time, perhaps most of the time, these services will come from inside the company. For many Marketcenters, there is an optimal mix of inside and outside services. With both types of service, the contract form of doing business acts as the business manager's main instrument of cost and quality control.

The service contract can also be used by top management to control its operations. When use of an internal service is made optional, the service is put squarely on its mettle. It must be able to perform competitively for the corporation's business managers or suffer the emotional and financial embarrassment from being bypassed. If internal services are consistently selected by the majority of business managers, they may comfortably presume that they are competitive in cost and quality. On the other hand, a significant rate of rejection is an equally clear sign that they are not doing their jobs.

Once they are positioned as competitive options, corporate support services are required to become Marketcenter oriented in the same way that business managers are required to become market driven. Every aspect of company operations can be geared to the same central source, customer needs. Development services take their directional cues from market needs. Their priorities are user priorities. They tend to build products that will be preferred. Production and promotion services are better able to serve markets through the business manager instead of serving only their parochial functional requirements.

Easing into Marketcentered Form

Marketcentering represents a major organization change. It has far-reaching operating implications. For the traditional product manufacturer who can benefit most from Marketcentering, it can be a major shock. Implementation by degree may be the strategy of choice. Along the way, a company can learn how much Marketcentering it can stand at any given time and what particular form it should ultimately adopt.

There are two effective ways of beginning the transition. One is Marketcentering a salesforce. The second is to create a separate marketing division to serve each major market. Both of these approaches can be used to precede complete Marketcentering.

Marketcentering a salesforce. Centering the sales function on a market requires a relatively minor up-front commitment and only a small number of alterations in the basic structure of a business. It nonetheless succeeds in establishing the central relationship of a market-driven organization: one-to-one contact between key customers by a single sales force that can prescribe the most cost-effective solution systems for their needs.

When a sales force is Marketcentered, each sales group within it is assigned a specific industry to serve. An industry information center becomes each sales group's principal resource. The sales group serves all the needs, or as many that are profitable to serve, of a group of key accounts. An account manager heads up each group much as the business manager of a full-fledged Marketcenter does. The account managers' responsibilities are focused on maximizing the profit contributions they bring to the customer account groups that are their "profit centers."

By concentrating a separate sales group on an industry, product-line selling becones transformed into industry-based selling. Petrochemical processors may make up one industry. Financial service institutions—banks, brokerages, and insurance companies—are another common industry grouping, as are government agencies and health care organizations.

A Marketcentered sales organization enables its sales teams to be knowledgeable about the markets in which they specialize. It also allows each of the markets to know more about the company whose sales specialists serve it and to perceive them as its specialist suppliers. Each sales group can sell an entire coordinated system of interrelated products and services instead of only a single product line. From the customer's point of view, a single sales contact provides access to the suppliers' sum total of solutions for a significant array of customer needs.

By selling solution systems through a single sales team, rather than selling individual products through many uncoordinated salespeople, a Marketcentered supplier can deal with comprehensive customer problems that would otherwise remain immune to single-product solutions. Larger packages can be sold. The seller's position vis-a-vis competition can also be made less vulnerable.

IBM is a company that has Marketcentered its sales function so that the sum total of information systems—computers, typewriters and word processors, telecommunications, copiers, and work stations—can be ordered from the same sales representative. The customers' needs, not organization boundaries, determine how they are served. Formerly salespeople from IBM's Data Processing Division, General Systems Division, and Office Products Division could converge on the same customer without ever coordinating with each other to solve the customer's overall business problems. Now an Information Services Group combines all IBM marketing and services. The group itself is segmented along market lines so that its full complement of offerings can be custom packaged for each industry's set of specific needs.

Marketcentering a Division. Centering a division to serve a major market requires regrouping parts of two or more product-defined or process-defined markets into a new single entity. At the same time, several products manufactured by traditional product manufacturing or processing divisions will have to be consolidated into single product families. While Marketcentering a sales force allows one sales group to serve an industry's needs with a package of several products and services, Marketcentering a division acts in an opposite manner. A range of essentially similar products based on different processes can now be targeted on a single user segment by the same division management.

Division Marketcentering is ideal for a company composed of multiple process technologies. Left to its historic organization form, it is inevitable that one division's provinces will be impinged on by other divisions as their product categories grow. Markets will then be served in a fragmented manner. Division sovereignties, along with their related jealousies over turf rights, will make it impossible for a company to dominate a market.

If, for example, a company simultaneously serves the pet food market from a dry-food processing division, a freeze-dried processing division, and a semimoist processing division, each division may be more competitive with its sibling divisions than with rival suppliers. Equally damaging, division managers under such a set-up may leave a no-man's land between their individual domains, creating gaps in product categories. These gaps can give competitors a clear shot.

General Foods is a classic example of the type of process-centered organization whose division structure can benefit from Marketcentering. Beverages used to be marketed by three divisions. If they were frozen, they were marketed by Birds-Eye. If they were powdered mixes, the Kool-Aid division marketed them. Breakfast drinks had to come from Post. No centralized attack on consumer beverage needs could be made. In a similar fashion, frozen puddings were marketed by Birds-Eye while Jell-O was the steward division for powdered pudding mixes. The pudding market had no dedicated representative within the company. Nor could the company address the total pudding market from a single source of supply.

A Marketcentered division can concentrate on correlating families of products made by different processing technologies but used by the same market segment. Three consumer product Marketcenters are shown in Figure 7.7. Each Marketcenter draws on the full range of corporate technologies. It derives support from the corporate service pool. Independently, it may carry out a small amount of product-connected market research and new product development. But its primary mission is to engage in "pure marketing."

Division Marketcentering improves the ability to dominate a complete category of market needs. A Marketcentered organization fosters a comprehensive solution capability by channeling multiple products into a market under a single sales drive. In advertising-intensive businesses, the cost-effectiveness of marketing can be significantly enhanced by coordinating promotion for several products against their common market.

A Marketcentered company grows by serving new needs in its established markets as a result of asking and answering the question, "What other needs of our key markets can we serve profitably?" At the outset of Marketcentering, each major market can be served more intensively. When growth on a broadened profit base becomes desirable, the same markets can be served more extensively by searching out their closely related needs and centering new businesses around one or more of them.

Growth Consulting

No business can grow alone. Customers therefore need a source for their growth. Since we cannot afford to leave customer growth to chance, nor can we wait for it to happen of its own accord, we must help our customers to grow if we are to be a growth business.

In order to grow customer profits and, by so doing, grow our own, we must restructure our key-account sales force. Sales personnel must be

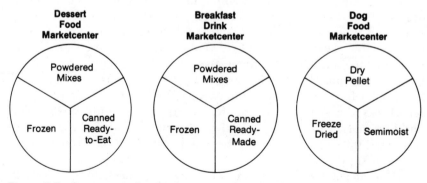

Figure 7.7. Consumer product Marketcenter.

positioned as consultative business growers for our major customers. The "product" they sell must be improved customer profit, a financial product composed of new assets, instead of their present physical product composed of processed costs. Improved profit is a derivative product. It is derived from the consultative application of physical products to a customer's business. When a customer cost center is reduced or eliminated by consultative product application, improved profit is derived. When customers can improve their sales revenues by applying our product, they can derive even more incremental profits.

Not only is the consultative product different, its sales strategy—how it is sold and to whom—is different, too. Higher level decision makers who manage customer business functions become buyers. It is they who are in the market for improved profit contributions from the functions they manage. Because their problems are defined in terms of contribution margin, net profit, and return on investment, considerations of our product's price and performance become subordinated to the financial values that we can add to a customer's bottom line.

The Three Criteria of Growth Selling

As with all financial services, the cost benefit of our consultative product applications will be judged by our customers on the basis of its impact on their profits. In other words, we will be evaluated as a consultant on the three how's of profit improvement:

1. *How much* do we help our customers to grow?
2. *How soon* do we provide them with new growth profits?
3. *How sure* can they be that we will be a dependable growth source for them?

These three criteria of how much, how soon, and how sure are the operating standards of a key-account sales force that sells by providing growth consultation to its major customers. The sales force must be able to win on at least two of the three criteria. If it offers much profit improvement to a customer, it must be prepared to make its delivery very sure. It need not deliver all of it soon. If it offers less, it must deliver both soon and sure.

The ability of our sales force to sell in this manner, to sell high-profit rewards at high-customer levels, is essential to growth because only high-value sales can yield the high margins that are essential for our own high profits. Two prior requirements must be met. First, an APACHE data system on the business problems and opportunities in our key customer accounts must be in place. Then our key-account sales force must be trained in the three basic Consultative Selling[4] skills of consultant positioning, profit-improvement proposing, and key decision-maker partnering.

Even before these two operating requirements become implemented, we will need to understand the new role of the key-account sales force as a growth tool. Instead of selling price-performance to purchasing-level managers, sales personnel will sell profit improvement at high levels. Instead of basing price on cost or competition, they will base their price on the value of the customer profit they improve. Instead of working from knowledge of their own business or competitive businesses, they will work principally from knowledge of their customer businesses. Instead of vending, they will consult.

How Consultative Salespeople Grow Customers

"I'm John Smith, your profit-improvement consultant," a consultative salesman begins his positioning with the top tier of a key-account customer. "My mission is to start today to work with you and your people in a close, continuing partnership to help improve your division's contribution to corporate profits by $1.5 million over the balance of this calendar year.

"I know that profit improvement for your division is your principal mission, too. That means that both of us now have in common your most important business objective: adding to your bottom line.

"I'd like to initiate our partnership by proposing to you the first of what will be an ongoing series of Profit Improvement Proposals that I will be putting together with the help of you and your people. This proposal, like the others that will follow, is designed to increase your revenues and reduce some of your costs by solving one of your persistent problems and taking advantage of a profitable opportunity.

"This first proposal is derived from homework we've been doing on your industry, your company, and your division. We've organized our homework into a database on your business. The database helps us pinpoint your major problems and opportunities, quantify their contribution to your costs, and then identify the single best solution for you. Our proposals come out of our database. They often allow us to zero in on the dollar amount of new profits you can expect when we solve one of your problems. The proposals also itemize the exact

---

[4]Consultative Selling is the registered trademark of the key account sales strategy invented by Mack Hanan.

strategies we will use to bring about the solution in your business that we are prescribing.

"Each strategy mix will be custom tailored to solve a specific problem. Before you decide to accept it, I will be able to prove to you and your people how much it will improve your profits and what the return on your investment will be. We will do all this in a cost-benefit analysis so we can study it, understand just where the profits we will add are going to come from, and use it as a form of 'spec sheet.'

"Before we affect your business in any way, we will both agree that the cost-benefit analysis is correct and that the system we have put together to solve the problem represents the optimal solution for you. Once we install a system, I and my support team will work with your operating people to monitor its progress in even further improving your profits. We will improve it further at once if we are able to. Later on, we may want to upgrade it to provide additional profit improvement.

"How long will we partner together in this way? For as long as you want us to help improve your profits."

Consultative Selling Disciplines

Vendors use traditional selling skills to move products on price, usually in high volume at low margins. Consultative business growers use an entirely different set of skills that enable them to penetrate top-tier decision points and create problem-solving partnerships with their decision-makers. They identify cost problems and sales revenue opportunities in customer businesses. They quantify their negative effects on profit. They then prescribe a solution. They quantify its additive effect on profit. They sell the difference. In this way, they are able to achieve the culminating objective of Consultative Selling: They base their price on the value of the customer's improved profit.

How can key-account sales representatives become positioned as consultative business growers? There is only one way. To be positioned consultatively demands that a sales representative sell from customer business knowledge. Customer data is the consultant's calling card: the ticket to high-level entry, to partnership with decision-makers and information sources and the basis for profit improvement proposing.

Consultative Selling is impossible without consultant positioning and the ability to partner on a win-win basis throughout a customer organization. The crunch discipline, however, is the skill of defining a customer problem quantitatively and calculating its solution in similar financial terms. This capability separates the true customer business growers who can actually improve customer profit from the hybrid "consultative vendors" who verbalize profits in narrative form but who never pay off in dollars and cents.

In this regard, the cost-benefit analysis shown in Figure 7.8 presents one form of the consultative salesperson's proof that a customer's profit can be improved. The accounting rate of return on the investment being proposed answers the question, "Is this the best deal?" The cost-benefit analysis acts as a test stand for the solution, allowing it to perform by generating cost and revenue units on paper in advance of its performance in actual operations. If a solution meets return-on-investment objectives in the cost-benefit analysis, it "works." Its growth contribution has been proved. Now all that remains to be done is to make it work operationally so that the proposed growth profits can start to flow.

Mutuality of the Growth Objective

Consultative Selling succeeds as a growth strategy where vending fails because vending is an adversary approach. It is win-lose. Price is the decisive element. If you pay my price, I win and you lose; if you pay less than my price, you win. Consultative Selling is win-win. If customer profit is improved through acquiring a premium value, supplier profit is improved through meriting a premium price that is commensurate with it.

Growth requires a mutuality of objective. We cannot grow for long by growing at customer expense. The more successful we are, the more certain it is that we will drive our customers out of business. Exploitation exploits the exploiter. For this reason, there is no push theory of growth. There is only pull theory that says the way to grow is to help our customers to grow. They will pull us along with them into accelerated growth.

How can we tell when our key-account sales representatives have acquired the ability to define mutual growth objectives with their customers? How can we determine when our representatives have become partners in mutual profit improvement? While there are many possible answers, there is one infallible signal. When our representatives are perceived by their customers as if they are *growth suppliers*, they have arrived as consultative profit improvers.

Growth Accounts

A growth account is a key customer, a heavy profit contributor, and therefore a crucial source of capital funding. Growth accounts are a priceless and often irreplaceable resource. New venture businesses must penetrate them as quickly as possible from the moment of their commercial onset. Established businesses must maintain them and grow with them.

INCREMENTAL INVESTMENT

1. Cost of Proposed Equipment/System $ _____
2. PLUS: Installation Costs   _____
3. PLUS: Investment in Other Assets Required   _____
4. MINUS: Avoidable Costs (Repairs & Remodeling)   _____
5. MINUS: Net After Tax Adjustment for Sale of   _____
        Properties Retired as Result of Investment
6. MINUS: Investment Credit   _____
7. TOTAL INVESTMENT (Sum of 1–6)   =======

COSTS-BENEFITS (Annual Basis)

	Proposal	Present or Competitive	±Difference
8. Sales Revenue	$ _____	$ _____	$ _____
9. MINUS: Variable Costs:	_____	_____	_____
10. Labor (Including Fringe Benefits)	_____	_____	_____
11. Materials	_____	_____	_____
12. Maintenance	_____	_____	_____
13. Other Variable Costs	_____	_____	_____
14. TOTAL VARIABLE COSTS (Sum of 10–13)	_____	_____	_____
15. Contribution Margin (Sum of 8–14)	_____	_____	_____
16. MINUS: Fixed Costs:			
17. Rent or Depreciation on Equipment	_____	_____	_____
18. Other Fixed Costs	_____	_____	_____
19. TOTAL FIXED COSTS (17 or 18)	_____	_____	_____
20. Net Income Before Taxes	_____	_____	_____

ACCOUNTING RATE OF RETURN ON PROPOSED INVESTMENT

21. Total Investment Cost (Line 7 or total $ _____
     Capitalized Annual Cost of System)
22. Net Income Before Taxes for Year (20) $ _____
23. Before-Tax Rate of Return (Line 22 ÷   _____
     Line 21)

Figure 7.8. Profit Improvement Proposal.

The importance of each growth account is threefold. First, it is a source of heavy ongoing profits, one of the 20 percent or so of all customers that provide up to 80 percent of profitable sales volume. Second, a growth customer is the most likely prospect for additional growth. Profitable business begets more profitable business. Third, the loss of a growth account not only cuts off the flow of current heavy profits but also the future heavy profits they would have helped to generate. It can also initiate a domino effect among other growth accounts, multiplying still further the dual loss of profits.

There is also a fourth impact that must be dealt with. It is always a costly and sometimes an extremely prolonged effort to try to regain the profit lost when a key account defects. No matter how large the expenditure, there is no assurance of success. Yet even if we succeed in replacing the loss, we may be no better off than when we began.

For any company, growth customers are relatively few in number, expensive and arduous to penetrate, always at risk because of their competitive allure, and absolutely vital. They deserve the best resources, the highest levels of care and attention, and the most dedicated planning. Next to growth plans as a whole, key account penetration plans are the most essential commitments. Like the growth planning process itself, growth account penetration plans merit a unique custom tailoring that will help insure early and continuing penetration.

Growth Account Criteria

A growth account has two definitions. It is a customer whose profit contribution is vital to our growth. It is also a business for whose own growth we are vital. To the extent that we abide by the second definition and concentrate on growing the businesses of our key accounts, they will in turn force us to grow with them.

Our proper concern as a growth business is to grow our customer businesses: not serve them, not stock them or supply them by selling to them but to help them grow. This dedication will create a partnering bond between us. It will be our common denominator with core markets, the basis for their ability to identify their successful profit-making with ours and to prefer us as their major source of supply.

We and our key customer accounts must enter into a growth conspiracy if we are to grow. We must know their growth plans and organize and operate to accelerate them. We must know the impediments to their growth and help overcome them. We must work with them to plan their growth with the same due diligence we use to plan our own growth. If they do not achieve their growth, neither will we achieve ours.

Looked at in this way, growth is revealed as a symbiosis. One company cannot grow. Growth requires two or more growers, each invigorating the other with new assets. Our assets come from the investments our growth customers make in our products, services, and systems. Their growth comes from the return we deliver on their investments with us.

Planning our growth means choosing our growth partners. What rationale should we use? We should form key-account relations with customers whose businesses we can most likely help to grow. They should make us their key supplier for the same reason, because they can best help us grow our own business. This mutuality of selection criteria insures our importance to each other and for the same reason.

The ability to grow a customer business should be our first cut at selecting key accounts. The ability of the customer to contribute to our growth is the second cut. If we reverse the rank order of these standards to put our own growth first, we will imperil our capability to form win-win partnerships with key customers. Their prior commitment is not to our growth but to their own. Only by embracing that same objective can we hope to partner with them.

Our ability to grow their business and their ability to grow our business need to be qualified by one additional consideration—the rate of our mutual growth acceleration. Because growth is a rate and not a state, we must be able to help our customers grow fast. The proof of fast growth is found in the rate of incremental profit that we can bring to our customers. The rate must be high. It must also be susceptible to sustained growth. The same qualifications apply to the customer's incremental contribution to our own business growth.

It is not simply growth itself that is the key account yardstick. Nor is it simply the rate of growth, which is a good deal more important. It is *the rate of growth of the rate of growth* that must be high and susceptible to progressive increase. When the growth of the rate of the growth rate slows, growth itself has slowed even though sales and profits continue to rise. This is the earliest warning signal that a growth phase may be ending for a key-account partnership or at least for one of the partners.

High Penetration Objectives

Are we a growth company? Only our key-account customers know for sure. If we are growing them and they are growing us at a high and increasing rate of growth, the answer is yes. This is the rock-bottom meaning of being market driven.

A key-account penetration plan is a device for harnessing our growth to our market's drive. How do we penetrate customers? We grow their businesses. How do we hold onto key accounts after initial penetration?

We grow their businesses even more. If we slow down or stop, we release our hold. A penetration plan should make it impossible for our grip to loosen without our awareness. It should also make sure we never forget that the name of the game with our major customers is mutual growth.

The penetration plan outlined in Figure 7.9 fulfills both of these requirements. It also provides a menu of growth strategies that will be applied to a customer to ignite the mutual profit improvement process. The plan quantifies "What's in it for the customer" and compares it with "What's in it for us." These profit commitments become each account manager's objectives. The specific Profit Improvement Proposals that will be implemented at major problem points in customer business functions become the plan's strategy mix—the investments that both we and our customers will make to achieve our objectives. Joint measurement, evaluation, and control procedures help insure achievement. An APACHE system forms the database.

Growth account penetration is driven by financial objectives expressed as two forms of contribution: the contribution that we are expecting to make to each account, which is the cause of the plan, and the contribution that the account is expected to make to us in turn. This is the result of the plan. By putting the customer's rewards first, we are making the plan customer driven from its cause—customer profits.

For both sets of revenue and profit contributions—from the account to us and from us to the account—we will want to know the most likely case numbers and how they differ from a year ago in the key index of rate of growth. We will also want to know the revenue-to-investment dollars required to produce the contributions and their ratio. This will indicate the productivity of the resource commitment that we have dedicated to support the contributions.

Our commitment to each key customer account must be ongoing. We must therefore plan our contributions for the next immediate year and the next following year so we have a rolling 3-year plan to manage every year. If we sell product and service systems whose installation and implementation will require 4 or 5 years before the customer or we can finally realize our full contributions, we can extend the penetration time frame accordingly.

Penetration Strategy Mix

Growth consulting takes the point of view that two strategic decisions are required to penetrate a key account. The first is how to position ourselves harmoniously with the account's business mode. If the account's mode is growth, we must sell in such a way that we help achieve incremental sales revenues or that we interpret our contribution in terms of incremental sales. For a growth customer, cost reduction is a much less compelling route to improved profits. If, on the other hand, an account is mature, we have the option to increase its sales revenues or decrease its costs. If it is declining, it will usually be more productive to treat it as a growth account by emphasizing incremental sales.

The second strategic decision is what to sell and to whom, organized on a problem-solution basis for the customer business functions we serve. The profit-improvement solutions we sell will act as our product

| | OBJECTIVES | | |
	Most Likely Case ($000)	+/− Difference Year Ago ($000)	Worst Case ($000)
1.1. Year 1 anticipated contribution TO account BY us			
Profit improvement by primary component of ROI to be affected:			
Costs	____	____	____
Sales	____	____	____
1.2. Year 2 contribution			
Profit improvement by primary component of ROI to be affected:			
Costs	____	____	____
Sales	____	____	____
1.3. Year 3 contribution			
Profit improvement by primary component of ROI to be affected:			
Costs	____	____	____
Sales	____	____	____
2.1. Year 1 anticipated contribution BY account TO us			
Profit	____	____	____
Sales revenues	____	____	____
Revenue-to-investment	__:__	____	__:__
2.2. Year 2 contribution			
Profit	____	____	____
Sales revenues	____	____	____
Revenue-to-investment	__:__	____	__:__
2.3. Year 3 contribution			
Profit	____	____	____
Sales revenues	____	____	____
Revenue-to-investment	__:__	____	__:__

Figure 7.9. Key Account Penetration Plan.

line. They will be our account penetrators. The partnerships we make with key business function decision makers will act as our data sources on customer problems and opportunities. The decisionmakers themselves will be able to act as our coaches—our "inside salespeople."

The creation of our strategy packages should be undertaken in person-to-person conjunction with the key decision makers in each customer account. After all, a penetration plan is a plan for improved customer profit as much as it is for our improved profit. Early and continuing customer participation in its creation will make it obvious that we are serious in our belief that our mutual profitability is indissolubly linked. Very often, we will find the enhanced data revelation that comes from shared planning will open up new problem areas to solve. Our partnerships will be strengthened, too, by working with key accounts before we propose or sell as well as by working in a more unified manner thereafter.

As our key-account penetration deepens and as our partnerships grow strong, we should consider sharing not just our strategy package but our entire plan with our customers. The very fact that we have a dedicated plan for their growth—a business plan in miniature—validates how significant they are to us. It is important that they know that. By revealing the contribution we expect from them, they will be able to appreciate how important they are to us. It is important that they know that, too. Rather than take advantage of that dependency, good business partners will work to keep us healthy as a guarantor of their own healthy profit growth.

Growth Partnering

Consultative Selling creates implicit partnerships with key-account customers. Growth partnerships create explicit partners, genuine joint venturers who agree to work together for a mutual share of new profits.

Growth partnering extends the Consultative Selling approach to its logical end point. The consultative sales representative says to the customer, "I don't want to sell to you anymore—I want to improve your profits." The growth partner says to the customer, "I don't want to sell to you anymore—I want to sell *with* you so that both of us can significantly improve our profits."

A growth partnership between a supplier and a user may be based on an informal joint selling agreement or may take the form of a new corporate enterprise, a third entity whose ownership, funding, and rewards are shared. It can be entered into on a specified short-term basis or it can run indefinitely on a 90-day cancellation clause. It can market a single product, service, and system, or several. It can take on complementary suppliers, thereby enlarging the system that will be sold and perhaps expanding the market opportunity as well.

Growth partnership potential is readily apparent between a component supplier and an original equipment manufacturer. Other forms of partnering can take place between two or more complementary manufacturers or service and maintenance suppliers, or with one of each. Both partners must bring to the party something the other partner needs in order to add major value to the offering and a joint marketing capability that can produce greater earnings than solo selling.

Typical Linkages

There are three main types of linkage for growth partners:

1. *Product plus product.* Joining two products is the simplest and therefore the most common basis for a growth partnership. The products should complement each other or one should extend the other's use. The two together can form a coherent unit, offering added value or a system designed to solve a comprehensive use problem. The product union must be sold to the same market already being served by at least one of the sales forces involved in the partnership, although not necessarily to the same decision-makers. A major impetus for a growth partnership is to be able to penetrate into higher buying levels because of its added financial impact on a customer's profits.

2. *Product plus sales force.* The second most common basis for joint partnering is to combine one supplier's product with another supplier's sales force. This gives the product supplier access to a professional sales organization. In turn, the sales force supplier gains access to another source of revenue. A variation on this theme provides a product supplier with access to a complete distribution channel, going beyond a sales force to include dealers and distributors, manufacturers representatives, sales agents, and retail outlets.

3. *Technical capability plus marketing capability.* A third partnership base brings together one partner's ability to develop, engineer, and perhaps manufacture with another partner's capability to market. In this case, more than a single specific product or even a family of products is provided. A good deal more than sales and distribution are involved in the marketing contribution. Each partner acquires a set of functional capabilities at which the other excels or can offer a significant cost-effective benefit.

Product partners may start with the union of their products and go on to link up the joint product package with one partner's sales force. A product-sales force partnership starts from a different base point. It is not two products that need each other for mutually accelerated growth. It is a product that needs incremental earnings from added outlets and a sales function that needs incremental earnings from additions to its line. Once consummated, these partnerships from different origins take on so many of the same attributes that the partners may become virtually indistinguishable.

The partnering of capabilities in science and marketing is much more future oriented than is linking up existing products with customer access. This type of partnership has attributes associated with classic joint ventures. Its impact is to provide an ongoing stream of science-based commercializations—not just one or two current products but several new products over a lengthy time frame—that represent significant market innovations.

For the technical partner, sales, distribution, and advertising capabilities are provided. Market data as the basis for research and engineering, demand-derived use values, and a value-to-price ratio for the heavy profit-contributor market segments are key benefits that flow from the marketer to the technician. The reverse flow can yield opportunities to drive into new markets or extend into existing markets with unique performance-based values.

Reduced Growth Requirements

Growth partnerships serve to reduce the requirements for obtaining new profits. They are one answer to the question, "What do we have to do in order to grow?" Their response is to say, "Less than we may have thought."

Growth partnering confronts the myth that growth requires a complete product line. One supplier's line can be "completed" by partnering with another. Their joint claim on distribution exclusivity or preferential retail stocking or shelving or advertising media dominance can be just as effective as if they were a single complete line supplier, and far less costly.

Nor does growth require sales force control. It is sales force compensation, not control, that determines push. Commissions, bonuses, and other forms of premiums can insure that high margin products are emphasized whether or not they are manufactured by the sales force's own company. The most overlooked incentive is training. It can give a sales force the tools for early entry and for faster close. It can also increase the comfort level for a sales force to get behind a new product and dedicate itself to it.

Growth does not require that every component of a product or service system be manufactured in-house. Manufacturers have always cared far more than their customers about complete system representation. Even the traditional fallback argument that it is cheaper to self-manufacture has not always been the case in many industries. Equally fallacious are beliefs that quality control must be loosened or lost if outside manufacture is engaged. Experience shows abundantly that both cost and quality standards can be maintained and even exceeded.

As the emphasis in marketing shifts away from providing performance benefits and persuading customers that "our benefits benefit best," the role of products will diminish. Marketing is increasingly an educational function. Its role is to teach customers less of what a product is and more of how to improve customer profit or productivity by implementing a product and service system. With customer profit as the focal point, the system will be evaluated less on its physical components and increasingly on its ability to prove its predicted contribution to a customer's bottom line improvement.

Going Operational

1. *Managing the partnership.* Growth partnerships must respect the ground rules for all partnerships. There are two partners, but there can be only one manager. Both partners must agree on whose manager will run the joint enterprise. He or she will be the "in charge" partner, responsible for mixing the combined resources in an optimal manner, planning their allocations, and reporting the mission as being on or off plan.

A partnership's manager must be market driven. As a general rule, this suggests that the manager will most likely be someone who has been well grounded in a marketing culture. He or she is more likely to be someone with a sales than a product or a technological background. The manager's major work will be to create the partnership's marketing plan. The plan will highlight mutually agreed objectives for profits. On behalf of the partnership, the manager must be responsible for achieving the objectives.

The manager's reporting system should be on a milestone-by-milestone basis, accounting for progress on an exception agenda. The manager reports to a small review team composed of representatives from both sides in the following disciplines:

a. Product managers of the products involved

b. The sales manager who is not acting as the partnership manager

c. Technical representatives of both sides

d. Financial representatives to track profit and insure value-based pricing

e. Data managers to structure the partnership's APACHE information base

2. *Compensating the partners.* The guiding principle for who gets what out of the partnership's profits is "to each according to his or her contribution." When both parters commit similar resources—planning, product, sales, and support services—a 50–50 split is equitable. In other partnerships, it is clear that one partner is the dominant member of the venture and should therefore be compensated proportionately.

If one partner contributes only a product, the other partner will play the dominant role. If one partner contributes only a sales force, the other partner will play the dominant role. If one partner contributes product, market data, and technological support while the other partner contributes the sales force, customer service, and financial support, the break will more nearly be half and half.

In many partnerships, the heavier contributor will also name the manager. This is essentially fair since the partner with the greater value of resources to protect should be given every consideration to ensure them. The ultimate consideration, though, should always be whose manager is more market driven.

3. *Growing the partnership.* Partnerships that work should be grown. There are two proven pathways to growing the original business of a growth partnership:

a. Migration. As soon as a partnership has established itself, opportunities should be explored to migrate the initial penetration. What additional markets can be penetrated with the same product combination? What additional products can be added to penetrate more deeply into the same market?

b. Multipartnering. The second set of questions to ask concerns taking on new partners. What other partners can be added to further complement the original product mix? What other partners can be added to help create a new product mix, either for the existing market or for new market penetration?

4. *Organizing the partnership.* Growth partnerships can take one of three organization forms. Figure 7.10 shows how they operate. In model 1, the most basic form of partnering, two companies sell enhancements provided by the other. In model 2, one company provides an enhancement that is sold by the other. A new company called C acts as a joint entity on behalf of both partners in model 3.

Marketing Considerations

In common with all enterprises, a growth partnership needs to be marketed internally to its own people and externally to its joint customers.

For both constituencies, the partnership requires a charter that answers the question, "What kind of animal is this?" The charter should set forth two sets of objectives. The first objective is the profit to be realized by the partnership's key-account customers. This must be expressed in terms of improved customer earnings or improved productivity if the partnership's market is not for profit. A sample profit objective might read, "To improve the incremental net profit of heavy users of small office systems by an average minimum of $10,000 NPAT per year." This sum should be significantly greater than either partner can deliver alone. The remainder of the statement of objectives will tell how the financial objective is to be achieved from a product and sales point of view.

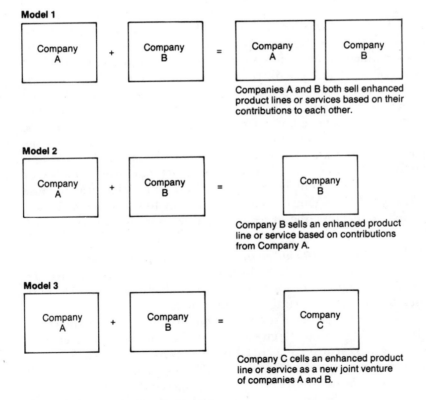

Figure 7.10. Growth partnering models.

The second set of objectives is the financial outcome to be realized by the partnership itself. This too must be expressed as improved profit. A sample objective might read, "To improve combined incremental net profit by a minimum of $500,000 per year." Each partner's split should be significantly greater than the profit from a comparable marketing investment as a lone supplier. The product, sales, technical, and marketing contributions of the partners fill out the remainder of the plan by telling how the financial objectives will be achieved.

The external objective comes first because it is the commanding objective. The internal objective is dependent on it. The external objective should be promoted vigorously. It is the partnership's basic market positioning tool, alerting customers to its commitment and targeting the partnership's ability to improve customer profit at a superior standard of value.

Business Implications

1. *Make or buy.*   For many companies, growth partnering is a make or buy decision in favor of buy. It provides a strategy for buying into a business through the contribution of resources. The alternative would be the commitment of much more sizable resources to make the partner's product or reproduce the distribution system in-house. The return for the lessened investment is a reduced reward. The eventual benefit is not necessarily the cost savings. It can be the prevention of opportunity loss by allocating the retained resources to still greater growth opportunities.

The buy option assumes importance in direct proportion to the capitalization that would be required by the make option. Partnering is therefore a growth strategy of choice for capital-intensive businesses or businesses contemplating entry into new distribution channels. Because it offers good leveraging, it is also a good way to test some of the key assumptions that underlie an acquisition decision in an industry in which fixed costs are predominant.

2. *Diversification without mortgage.*   Growth partnerships are miniature user-friendly business diversifications. They permit diversity without mortgaging a company's assets, cannibalizing its existing businesses, or adversely affecting its balance sheet.

The forgiveness aspect of diversification through growth partnerships is twofold. Partnerships forgive the entry fee required for diversification. They make it affordable. In addition, they forgive an expensive and embarrassing public exit if the venture fails to work out. Disengagement provisions can be built into the partnership agreement so that divestiture is free from mortification or acute financial disadvantage to either party.

3. *Market research effect.* A growth partnership is a living market research probe. It tests the existence of a market opportunity, qualifies its constituents, and quantifies the amount of profitable sales volume they will be able to contribute.

It is an excellent market test, with unquestioned validity. It also avoids questions about whether or not its findings are projectable.

In the course of its operation, the partnership builds a database on its joint market's composition, needs for profit and performance improvements, product usage, competitive transactions, and future plans. The database is the reservoir of the partnership's decisions. Its knowledge content can also become a marketable product in itself, packaged and sold to a variety of noncompetitive suppliers, media, research organizations, financial institutions, and consultants.

4. *Management experience.* To partner with another company gives management on at least one side—on both sides if the partnership represents a business diversification—a learning experience about a new business. This can be a priceless value. It is especially valuable for a business that has remained in a single industry for most or all of its commercial life and is inexpert or uncomfortable confronting diversity.

A subsidiary advantage falls to the individual managers who represent each of the partners in the venture. They get a taste of what it means to be more entrepreneurial—to lead a new business venture and penetrate a market that may itself be new. Growth partnerships grow managers as well as businesses. Since a manager's life cycle can be as much as 5 times the growth cycle of a single business entity, manager growth may be the most important long-term reward of the growth partnership strategy.

Growth partnerships between suppliers and customers and even between two or more nominal competitors are forms of shared sales expansion. Other types of partnering join a mature company with an entrepreneurial business, any number of partners in collaborative research and development, and partners in discovery whose objective is educational rather than operational.

Mature Company— Entrepreneur Company Partnerships

Young, innovative companies may find it beneficial to enter into one or more partnerships with mainstream industrial or technology companies as a means of hastening their diversification. At the point in their development cycle at which they have established themselves in their entry business and are well financed to carry it forward, their entrepreneurial interest often turns to next-stage migration opportunities. A large company can provide research funds for the discovery of second-stage diversifications that do not dilute the financing for the entrepreneur's base business.

Some of the discoveries may become new entrepreneurial businesses for the innovative company. Others may become ventures or joint ventures for the mature partner. On occasion, the original business may become a candidate for the older company's acquisition while its entrepreneur moves laterally to start up an adjacent business concept.

These relationships are often loose or light at the outset, much less structured than a joint venture or minority buy-in investment. This feature gives the entrepreneur breathing room and keeps the larger company less committed in the eyes of its board and the investment community. At the same time, it gives the company a chance to explore a growth area under the guidance of one of its pioneering pacesetters, to develop a database on potential business prospects, and to provide some of its managers with firsthand experience in observing entrepreneurial business-building sensitivities at work.

Research and Development Partnerships

Within individual companies and by means of pools of several companies, a strategy of R&D partnering is a means of enabling new money to be brought into their development processes. Through an R&D partnership, external private investment is invited to fund corporate research and development on the bet that new high-profit products will yield an above-average return to the investors. The companies they invest in expect to benefit by acquiring new businesses based on their newly funded developments as well as on superior new earnings.

Another type of R&D partnership is the technology development venture such as MCC, the Microelectronics and Computer Technology Corporation. MCC is owned and operated by the several companies that compose it: Advanced Micro Devices, Control Data, Honeywell, Motorola, NCR, National Semiconductor, and RCA, among others, all of whom will be contributing technical talent to develop new ultrasophisticated computers and software, integrated circuit packaging, and computer-assisted design and manufacturing.

These are technologies that all the consortium's members hope to be able to use as the foundation for developing their own individually designed products and services. If the joint partnership works as planned, each of the contributing companies will significantly reduce the cost, time, and risk of development and lower the ratio of their individual capital investments. Wasteful duplication of scarce development funds and even more scarce scientific and technical talent may also be lessened by the operations of MCC.

Discovery Partnerships

Companies whose mainstream technologies have run out of growth potential, and even growing companies in high-technology industries whose sciences quickly burn out in fad-type cycles, are pooling resources to discover technologies and markets of the near-term future. In some cases, they are trying to spot emerging technologies and market segments whose opportunity windows are just opening. Other partnerships are interested in getting a grasp on the entry requirements imposed by new technologies or the probable size and longevity of growth markets in which neither partner has had experience. In one way or another, they are trying to get a handle on the future.

8
Growth Strategy for Participation

There are two ways to fund growth. We can invest in our ability to grow, buying asset bases for ourselves. Or we can invest in someone else's growth. We can buy into it as a minority investor. Or we can buy it out as an acquirer. Either way, we can participate in the growth of businesses that, even though technologically diverse, have a current relationship to "our game" or that may possess a future relevance.

External investment expands our growth horizon. We can take a range of positions from minority investor to owner in several companies, some of which may be based on newly emergent technologies that are still below the horizon in terms of their commercialization. Our investments can give us early positioning in potential big-winner ventures, providing a toehold from which we can enlarge our involvement or step back without major sacrifice. They can also provide us with the opportunity to learn new sciences and markets without having to be in them ourselves while we decide whether or not we want to be.

Some managers regard external growth investments as an extender, giving them a reach into developmental businesses that they themselves cannot source or afford. Other managers see it as a safety net that can give them a fallback position in case internal investments fail to yield a productive return. Still other managers want to be involved with what the outside world is doing as a learning experience so they can get the feel of a business without making a full-scale commitment. In the case of emergent technologies, managers may want to position themselves with several of them until it becomes clear which scientific variation and which management team will be the survivors.

Growth strategy calls for participation as a minority owner of a small number—two to five—of entrepreneurial businesses in technologies that are potential supplements to our existing products or systems or that have the capacity to obsolete them or that can become the superior profit-makers of the near-term future. Our initial participation should not, as a rule, exceed a 20-percent stake. This will allow us to make several such investments, spreading our risk as well as opening us up to greater rewards. Maintaining our ownership at a minority level will also discourage us from meddling in a venture's operations to the point at which, given more control, we could easily smother it in the crib.

Meanwhile, we have our foot in the door. We are poised to enlarge our role, up to and including the option to acquire. And all the time we are learning. What does it take to be in this kind of business? What type of management? What type of technology? Where are the problems, the pitfalls, and the bugs? Who are the main players? What are the markets and how can they be grown? What are they willing to pay for growth? What are their options and how do they compare?

A minority investment is a box seat on the future. At a cost proportional to an internal investment, putting money into someone else's business gives us a leg up on an industry's life cycle. Instead of starting from ground zero, we are already up and running. If we make our bets wisely, we will have relationships with the best management teams in a burgeoning industry—the ones who will not only make it but make it big. Everyone else will want them too. But we will have the inside track. If we were to wait, we might have to put our money into a second-rate company or buy a much smaller position in the one we want at a significantly higher premium. The worst case is that we could be frozen out of an emerging growth business completely.

General Motors is an example of investment foresight. In order to remain competitive in the global automobile market, GM must reduce its labor content per car. Automation is its only answer. Labor must be replaced by machines that will replicate human beings. The solution is robots. They will need to have programed brains to tell them what to do. They will also need sensory skills in order to execute what their brains tell them. As a result, GM has made minority investments, usually below the 20 percent level and frequently in more than one company in the same field: an 11 percent investment in artificial intelligence through Teknowledge and a 15 percent investment in it through Applied Intelligent Systems; an 18 percent investment in robot vision through Robotic Vision Systems and a 15 percent investment in it through View Engineering. As these businesses mature, GM can exercise options to buy more, buy out, or cash out.

The GM approach gets the company in at an early time in a

technology's life. Its opportunity window is just opening. Venture businesses need capital. They may also need support services; some may even need a real-world test stand for their first products and an assured first customer thereafter. As GM is ensconced in the catbird seat, its competitors are denied access.

In the case of General Motors, selecting emergent technologies in which to invest fits a pattern. They match up with GM's requirements for its automobile business. But what if growth can only come from new businesses—technologies and markets in which our current asset base provides no foundation in expertise, experience, or rationale? How then can we choose our investment partners?

A two-part method can put a value on the future worth of a minority investment. First, growth industries are assessed. Then, within them, assessments are made of individual growth candidates.

Assessment of Growth Industries

1. *Industry databasing.* The first step in future valuing is to create a database on high-growth industries. Its purpose is to determine whether growth promise is rampant in an industry or not. This sets up the growth universe.

Two issues need to be resolved before data gathering. One is how an "industry" is to be defined. How broad should the definition be—the entire controls industry, for example, or only the process controls industry? Within process controls, should the focus be on food industry processing controls or chemical industry processing controls? The more vertically narrow the defintion, the easier, faster, and less costly the database will be.

The second issue is how to measure "growth opportunity." Should it be valued in comparison with GNP growth or with the projected growth of a company's own industry? Should it be compared with alternative opportunities offered by other growing industries?

A growth industry database should contain information on the estimated nature and size of the industry's opportunity to grow, the time frame for its most rapidly accelerated growth, the technical and marketing capabilities required to grow the markets that will be the industry's chief sources of growth, constraints against growth and their timing, and next generation migration opportunities for companies in the industry to further diversify their growth.

A menu of information for a growth industry database is shown in Figure 8.1.

Item number 3 on the menu, the key customer markets that will source profits, is the most frequently neglected. Yet, as hindsight will invariably show, it is the single most important predictor of industry growth. Only if an industry's customer markets are growing will the industry itself to be able to grow.

Where does growth data come from? There are three main sources. One is the information that is already known or knowable inside our own company. It is in our existing business databases or in the heads of our people. A second source is publicly available data from industry, business and trade associations, investment houses, government studies and reports, the business press, studies by research organizations available by purchase or subscription, books, and consultants. Finally, there is primary research that will have to be specifically commissioned.

2. *Primary research.* The second step in future valuing is to pene-

1. Nature and size of growth trends, patterns, and projections on a 5-year time frame
2. Allied industry growth trends
3. Key customer markets that will source profits.
    3.1. Customers
    3.2. Suppliers
4. Key skills, capabilities, and resources determining the ability to acquire profits
5. Chief constraints on profit
    5.1. Availability and sophistication of supplemental technologies
        required for cost-effectiveness or second-generation migration
    5.2. Legislation
    5.3. Energy or scarce labor and materials dependencies
    5.4. Market uncertainties, education requirements, or limitations
    5.5. Competition
        5.5.1. Directly competitive technologies
        5.5.2. Potential end-run preemptive technologies
        5.5.3. Entry dues for new competition
6. Key competitor factor analysis
    6.1. Key manufacturers
        6.1.1. Market shares and positions
        6.1.2. Major sources of revenues per product per market
        6.1.3. Major costs per functional cost center
    6.2. Key customer markets per manufacturer
    6.3. Key product lines per manufacturer per market
        6.2.1. Product benefits
        6.2.2. Price-performance ratios
    6.4. Sales and distribution patterns per product per market
    6.5. Customer purchase and use patterns per product per market
7. Second-generation migration opportunities for current technology

Figure 8.1. Growth industry analysis.

trate directly into the markets in which high growth is happening or is anticipated. There is no substitute for this type of up-to-the-minute firsthand information whose data can be structured exactly the way it is required.

Every primary research study is unique. Nonetheless, certain generalities must prevail.

As a start, up to five industries can be evaluated at the same time. If an industry's component segments are unknown at the outset, a principal objective of the research must be to identify them. When they are known from the outset, or at least strongly suspected, research should proceed segment by segment.

Within each industry segment, two types of companies should be studied. One is the leading-edge businesses. These are the fast growers. To counterpoint their peculiarities, a smaller number of more typical companies should also be assessed. Through personal interviews—up to perhaps a dozen or so per company—management executives, operating officers, R&D and systems engineers, and manufacturing and marketing representatives should be engaged in question and answer dialogues. Management information directors and database managers can also be important research sources.

A minimal list of what is learnable includes the following seven categories:

a. Size and scope of the current business base

b. Prospective rate and extent of 1-to-3-year future growth

c. Nature and intensity of customer needs

d. Customer willingness to pay for benefits in terms of typical value-to-price relationships

e. Market estimates of yet unfilled needs and ideal benefit concepts

f. Keystone elements in the technology, along with the perceived barriers to technological improvement and the expected advantages of rival technologies and competitive suppliers

g. Market assay of current and prospective suppliers

These categories of inquiry are designed to shed light on the two principal areas of knowledge necessary to estimate future value. One is the market. This is first and foremost. Without understanding its size, scope, needs, and values, no technology that would pretend to serve it is comprehensible. Second, of course, is the technology itself. Since future deployment is the prime need to know, emphasis is placed less on the state of the art today and more on what its opportunities and barriers may be for ongoing development and its liablity for near-term preemption.

When the full complement of information has been gathered, it should be summarized into a consensus. One or more scenarios can be constructed around its most salient points. It is then useful to pursue a modified Delphi approach, returning the scenarios and consensus findings to the respondents and inviting a reevaluation of their initial answers. In some cases, Delphi playback can take place a second or even third time around.

Assessment of Growth Candidates

Industry databasing spiked by specific primary research constitutes the foundation for assessing growth technologies. The next step in future valuing is to identify leading-edge suppliers, smoke out the sleepers, and analyze each one intensively according to the criteria in Figure 8.2.

In addition to these eight standards, there is a ninth yardstick that is somewhat more subjective than the others and, in the end, may be the ultimate determinant of what action will take place. It is the sense of fit, how a candidate company's style of doing business jibes with our own management style and our concept of how a business should be run. Each technology brings with it a specific business style. Over the long run, the capability of two management styles to be compatible often turns out to be the central capability in an acquisition. Unless it exists, none of the other capabilities may ever be fully realized.

To build an accurate profile of a leading-edge supplier or one with potential "leading edge-ability," eight sources of information can come into play to supplement facts that are obtained from a candidate company itself:

1. Industry consultants
2. Lawyers and bankers
3. Investment analysts
4. Credit sources
5. Trade associations
6. Trade publication editors
7. Suppliers
8. Competitors

Market analysis should be the critical dimension of an individual candidate's critique. Technical analysis should be second. Even though it is the technology that will be the alleged reason for an acquision, market opportunity is the prize that will, in the final analysis, be acquired.

Technology is the means, not the end, of obtaining new profits. By itself, it represents a cost. Only when it can be commercialized through market demand can it begin to make a contribution to profits.

In the typical acquisition situation, financial analysis is largely employed to validate past value. The track record of a candidate becomes crucial. The assumption is made that a mangement with a history of knowing how to make money will continue to make money. The future can then be projected from the past. In reality, however, very little of the

---

1. Industry position
   1.1. Present position
   1.2. Most likely 3-year position
      1.2.1. If unacquired
      1.2.2. If acquired by us (= added value from our acquisition)
2. Management base
      2.1.1. Entrepreneur analysis
      2.1.2. Support staff analysis
      2.1.3. "Fit" compatibility evaluation
      2.1.4. Acquirability evaluation
3. Financial base
      3.1.1. Sources of financing
      3.1.2. Dollar value of earnings and revenues
      3.1.3. Critical ratios
4. Technology base
      4.1.1. Patent or other proprietary basis
      4.1.2. Competitive differentiation
      4.1.3. Growth migration potential
5. Market base
      5.1.1. Key market analysis per segment
      5.1.2. Key customer accounts per segment
6. Product Line base
      6.1.1. Key products per market segment
      6.1.2. Price-performance ratios per product
      6.1.3. Systems capability
      6.1.4. Innovative capability
7. Sales and distribution base
      7.1.1. Present channels
      7.1.2. Potential channels
         7.1.2.1. Agents
         7.1.2.2. Representatives
         7.1.2.3. Dealers and distributors
8. Strategic growth base
      8.1.1. Anticipated changes in industry
      8.1.2. Anticipated impacts on candidate
      8.1.3. Anticipated critical issues for candidate
      8.1.4. Optimal strategy mix for candidate

Figure 8.2. Growth candidate analysis.

past can be acquired. The future will rarely be a straight-line projection, especially in high-growth industries with accordion-like life cycles caused by the rapid-fire rate of innovation.

The discovery of currently high profits and good cash flow may signal quite the reverse of high future value. These signs may be danger signals. They may warn that an industry is topping out or, at the very least, that a candidate is moving away from its growth phase and entering maturity. If so, its rate of future growth may be progressively reduced.

Two checkpoints of financial analysis are relevant to future valuing. One is prospective cash flow analysis, with emphasis on worst-case analysis—not best case. Growth should not be assumed. Quite the contrary, a business should be forced to show cause that it will continue to grow. A second index is rate of growth as distinguished from growth itself. In projecting growth, slope is the key. Growth itself may continue. Profits may go on at a high level. Industry sales leadership may be maintained. But once the rate of growth slows, the heyday of money-making can quickly pass. The rationale for an acquisition under these circumstances will undergo change. So will its value-to-price ratio. And so will the contribution it can be expected to make to future profits.

The Upshot of Future Valuing

The upshot of this two-stage method of valuing future worth—assessing growth industries and then evaluating individual growth candidates within them—is a nogo/go decision on a per-industry, per-candidates basis.

A nogo decision is the beginning of more hard work. Its message is twofold: look elsewhere or revise our criteria, perhaps both. A go decision should have two components:

1. Go with (*a*) these specific product lines (*b*) at these price-performance ratios (*c*) sold through these channels (*d*) at these value-to-price ratios (*e*) with these margins (*f*) to these key customer market segments.

2. In order to obtain these specific product lines, (*a*) acquire this technology (*b*) under these terms and conditions (*c*) within this time frame (*d*) at this price (*e*) with these expectations of its flow of future values.

Some companies structure this information in the form of a growth plan that they prepare on behalf of each acquisition candidate. The plan acts as a trial balance, allowing the acquirer to play a "What if" game with the candidate's business. What if we owned it—how much money could we expect it would most likely earn? When? At what cost? With what? From whom? For how long? What then?

PART 4
The Growth Mindset

9

Growth Parables

In growth, there is pain without gain. Losing always hurts more than winning. But there is no gain without pain. Pitfalls and pratfalls abound. There are more ways not to grow than to grow. It is only natural for us to find them and apply them, thinking them to be rare and that our discovery of them is nothing less than magic. Only later do we learn that we have unwittingly replicated someone else's no-growth or slow-growth strategy that, true to itself, was a failure then and will be a failure again now.

We learn that success and failure generally announce themselves quickly. The "eight-barrel pumpers" that are neither—but that permit the perception of promise—are the problem children of growth. On the one hand we are counseled to cut our losses and run. On the other, we are told to hang in. Usually we hang in. Our direct losses mount. So does our opportunity loss. Yet it is true that just often enough one person's eight-barrel pumper becomes another's gusher.

The pain of cutting and running, and the pain of hanging in, have produced the gain of growth parables, a small number of hard-won pithy lessons that are conducive to real growth. If we heed them, the parables can help us to avoid the waste of resources, especially the people skills that are the major cost of growth strategy, and to capitalize on the fleeting openness of our windows of opportunity.

Three parables probably sum up 80 percent of the lessons of growth. They are concerned with risk and its minimization, maturity and its avoidance, and success factors and their fewness.

Time and Distance
Dictate Risk

Time is the enemy of growth. If a business is to grow, it must grow fast, against time. Growth must begin at the moment of penetration and proceed at a rising rate: not only the *rate of growth* must be fast but the *rate of growth of the rate of growth* must also be fast and significant.

The time to commercialization, to the commencement of cash flow, is critical to growth strategy because the counterforces to growth breed in time. Given enough time, a market will solve a problem or shift its preference for the solution. We may be too late with too little. Its priorities may move, reducing us to a postponable consideration rather than a necessary one. Time allows competitors to mobilize, offering similar solutions at a more preferable return on a customer's investment. Time also fosters the onset of successor technologies that may outmode us by hurdling our basic science or rendering it less cost effective.

While we prepare to go commercial, we are held hostage by our markets, our competitors, and the life cycle of our technology. Can we make them all stand still long enough to make our entry, catch our curve, and preempt our share? The only chance we have is to be first, to be fast, and to compress time by our haste to market.

The bonus of being fast is that we may be first. It has its disadvantages. We will have to educate our market. In the process, we will also educate our competitors so that their learning curves will be accelerated and their growth plans can draw from our own. But the upsides of being first outweigh these problems. To be first is to make the market. We can define it, create it in our image, become its standard of value against which all latecomers must be compared, and even give it our name. We can plow deep while others sleep.

Entering a market anew incurs a high degree of difficulty. Its inertia must be overcome, its attention focused, and its consciousness raised. But entering a mobilized market that is defended by a prior source of supply that has partnered with its customers is a greater difficulty by far. Confrontation may be cost ineffective. Attrition will defeat fast growth. Only a flank attack against a marginal niche may be left open. If the niche market has a low-growth potential, first may remain foremost.

In growth strategy, distance lends disenchantment when it is distance from our core technologies and marketing capabilities. When a business sets out to grow, its managers learn soon enough that there is no such thing as universal management skill. A good manager cannot manage any business. We are all bound to our databases: what we know about our markets and the technical and marketing capabilities required to serve them. As we increase the distance from our database to penetrate lesser known markets or sciences, we increase our risk. The further we go, the less we know and the harder it is to grow.

Growth by logical extension from an existing technology is safer than growth by diversification into new technologies. Growth by logical extension from an existing market into adjacent markets is safer than growth by new market entry. As growers, we are what we know. In the final analysis, we will grow only as much as our knowledge of how to use our technology and marketing abilities to help our customers grow.

When we can no longer play "our game"—when we are unable to grow customers by reducing the costs in their business functions that we know how to reduce or by increasing their sales revenues in markets whose needs we know—we are in trouble. We have outrun our knowledge supply. We cannot grow anyone. We can only supply them with products and services at vendor prices. We may be able to build a business. But we will not be able to grow it.

Successful diversification is databased. It starts with a market of needers who cannot be served by existing technology or marketing capabilities. Their costs cannot be significantly reduced. Their sales cannot be significantly increased. As a result, their profits cannot be significantly improved. A new science must be acquired, or a relationship formed with it, so that we can produce products whose performance can bring the desired cost reduction or sales increase. Marketing abilities or relationships must be added to our asset base that can provide new sales or distribution capability. This is how sensible growth takes place: when asset base-building follows market need-seeking so that growth is databased from its inception.

Assets are never the source of growth. They are the result of our requirement for new capabilities to meet market needs. Through their needs, markets are our growth source. They cause our capabilities; they are our drivers.

Maturity Is the Curse of Growth

Markets are growth's cause. Maturity is its curse. As a business matures, either because its market can no longer be grown or because its technology can no longer grow it, the key index of growth—its rate—slows. The rate of return of each incremental dollar that is invested in the business enters decline. There are better things to do with our money. From our customers' point of view, there are better things to do with their money than invest it with us. The reason is the same. The rate of return can be improved by investing elsewhere.

Maturity is growth's antagonist, not simply a successive stage in the business life cycle but the very antithesis of a high rate of profit-making. "Our game" of how we grow customers has entered the late innings. Our growth strategy has grown old, albeit still workable, still marketable, and still justifiable. But profits will not flow into us again at the annual minimum rate of 20 percent that is the floor for growth.

Sooner or later, all businesses become mature. Every day that its onset can be postponed—that maturity can be held off—is another irreplaceable day of growth profits. Delaying maturity must be a principal objective of growth strategy. There are two ways in which it can be accomplished.

For each individual line of business, growth policy must insure its position as its market's standard of value. No one must be able to do better what it does to help its markets grow. Its abilities to improve customer profits must become, and remain, the industry norms for squeezing costs out of business functions or extracting new sales revenues from customer markets. If norm control is lost, the loss of margin control will not be far behind. That is the full meaning of what it is like to be mature: Our margins come into the command of our markets. Thereafter, our customers will grow themselves at our expense, by manipulating our price. We will be depositioned as their prime or exclusive growers and become one of their alternate vendors.

If we manufacture and market families of businesses, our growth policy must provide for a continuing generation of S-curves. Each curve will be a potential growth business, a branded product, service, or system that has high unit margin capability because it has the ability to grow customers at a high rate. Even before we produce a new S-curve, we know in advance the compression from competition and technology that will telescope its period of maximum profitability. We must acknowledge our concern by a tripartite approach. For every brand on the table that is currently serving a market, we must have two more. One must be in the oven, becoming table-ready. The other must be in the mixing bowl becoming oven-ready. This is our defense against coming up empty.

In the event that maturity comes to our table, we can go to our oven for a replacement brand. If our oven brand stops growing prematurely, we have recourse to our mixing bowl. Our assembly line for developing S-curves will be in swing.

This concept of our growth commitment is designed to circumvent being a one-shot grower. Along with the reliability of our profit-improvement skills, the continuity of our primacy in applying them must be our second quintessential quality. It is our guarantor of survival as a growth business. This is not to say that markets will not do business with one-shot growers. Of course they will. But they will do so only once. In this way, more memorable case histories will be built than will growth businesses.

Success Factors Are Few but Powerful

When successful growth strategy is dissected, the post mortem findings are always the same. A very small number of all its components account for most or all of the success. Failed strategy reveals the same preponderance of a critical few factors. When growth strategy fails, it is generally one or, at most, two factors that have been largely responsible. In the case of its PC_{jr}, IBM made two crucial errors: It misjudged who would buy it and how much they would be willing to pay. These are really one and the same. The answer to who will buy it is the market that is willing to pay a premium price to be grown. If there is no answer, as there was not, there is no market.

Success factors exemplify the 80-20 rule. Fewer than 20 percent of all strategy components contribute the *sine qua non* of growth. If we do these things and do them well, we will probably grow regardless of what else we do not do or do poorly. The converse is also true. If we do not do these things or do them poorly, we will probably not grow regardless of what else we do or do well.

Growth, like all strategy, is essentially minimalist in nature. It requires our concentration on a small number of drive forces and a benign neglect of their dependent variables. Growers of businesses need not, therefore, be well-rounded strategists. Quite the contrary, they must be angular and pointedly focused on their main chances.

Of all the factors that attend growth, some causing it and others coinciding with it or being companionate with its central success elements, three are indispensable. They bring the power to grow:

1. *Entrepreneur management.* Provides the driver for growth whose objective is proft, whose time frame is tight, and whose market sensitivity is ultrasharp.

2. *Marketing skills.* Provide the driver and the drive team with the agility to penetrate a market with a premium value in return for a premium price and thereby brand their business.

3. *Emergent technology.* Provides the capability to create the premium performance values that, in turn, create the premium profit values by which customers are grown.

Bring an entrepreneur manager possessing marketing skills together with an emergent technology and we will have the power source for growth. Each is critical. All three are interdependent, making them synergistic when they are in parallel with each other and thereby multiplying their power.

What do the three growth parables teach us? They tell us the touchstones to growth. They say that we must grow fast, beating competition to the punch and staying one step ahead of maturity. They say we must grow based on what we know about how to grow our customers, making certain that we do not reach beyond our grasp of market fact. They say that we must have 80-20 growth, putting our money on a small group of the most powerful growth forces and fighting off distraction and dilution of our resolve.

If we learn these lessons, we can reduce the negative impact of the failure factors that work against growth: growing slowly and missing our windows of opportunity, ignoring or outrunning our databases, and trying for excellence across the board or in irrelevant preoccupations instead of being narrow, repetitive, and dedicated where it counts. Failure is hard to cope with. But it is more frequent than success because its process is more compatible with our preconceptions of "what should work." Success is far less comfortable while it is in process. We are basing so much on so little and so few. But the result is sweet and makes our perseverance, but only in retrospect, seem perfectly natural.

Only when we have grown does it seem to have been "the only way." If there were a fourth growth parable, it would be this.

10
Grow-Think

Growth is a thinking process about markets. If we think about our technologies, we will not grow. If we think about our products, we will not grow. If we think about our competitors or their technologies and products, we will not grow. We will grow only if we think about the sources of our growth—our markets. In order to grow, we must be *market-thinkers*.

What we think about our markets and *how we think* about them are the keys to our success. We must be preoccupied by the growth of our markets and how we can accelerate it. That will force our thinking onto the strategies we need for our own growth. And we must think in certain ways about our strategies in order to optimize them.

We must think *centrically* about our strategies, concentrating on our markets.

We must think *inversely* about our strategies, beginning with our markets instead of ending with them.

We must think *minimally* about our strategies, matching but not exceeding our market's needs.

We must think *preemptively* about our strategies, offering premium solutions to our markets' problems.

We must think *pithily* about our strategies, refining them to the 20 percent that will give us the 80 percent of our growth.

These are the five components of market-think, the thinking process about the markets that source our growth.

Thinking Centrically

Growers must be concentrators. This does not mean thinking hard. Concentration means the application of main strength at the few most crucial points of a business. It is the ultimate application of the 80-20 rule.

To practice concentration, growers must train themselves to get to the center of the most central issues that determine growth. Concentration is centrical thinking; it applies main focus at central points. In this way, growers can make certain they are attending to the truely crucial issues. At the same time, they can ignore the infinite and often tempting distractions of pernicious peripherals.

Because of the need to concentrate, managing a growing business—unlike running a mature business—is an unbalanced process. Growth skews attention to the smallest number of supercritical strategies that determine success. If these are managed wrong, it will not matter what else is managed right. If everything else is managed right and the few supercritic strategies are managed wrong, the things that are managed right will not matter.

Centrical thinking is convex. It focuses on what is vital. All else becomes secondary, to be ignored by the grower who can be secure in the knowledge that it will not matter very much to the final result.

Day-to-day business is a conspiracy against concentration. Its demands diffuse our attention. Our technology fascinates us. We are preoccupied by it. Our competitors concern us. We are paranoid about their capabilities and give ourselves over too easily to excess about their intentions. All customers challenge us. We are committed to selling them at any cost and at any price. We invest 80 percent of our time and treasure in pursuit of the sales that yield only 20 pecent of our profits. Conversely, we fail to focus on the 20 percent of our people, our products, and our purchasers who contribute 80 percent of what we earn.

We plan to be strong everywhere. As a result, we are strong nowhere. We refuse to lose any sale no matter how profitless. As a result, we lose sales that could be the most profitable. We know everything that is knowable about the features, functions, and benefits of our products, but we know less than is knowable about the profit impact they can make on our customers' businesses. As a result, we sell performance values instead of profit values and we trade off more and more performance for less and less price.

We manage every product line no matter how small its contribution. We train every sales representative. We advertise to every purchasing agent. We service every sale. We lose our concentration and, along with it, we lose our profit.

Management is as much a process of renunciation as focus. Without renunciation of the peripheral sources of our profits, there can be no concentration on its primary sources. These are always few in number. The fact that this is so makes growth possible. Being few, we can put our minds to them, our resources against them, and our reputation on our expertise in managing them.

Thinking Inversely

Plannable growth starts with market opportunity. The eventual end users are the initial growth providers. Sooner or later we will have to deal with them. If we make our deal later, after our instincts and intuition have had their way with us, we invite the end user to be our judge.

End users are stern judges. They condemn our attempts at growth. Not, they say, at my expense. If, however, we make our deal sooner, we can invite the end user to be our partner. Partners, not judges and the judged, grow businesses.

If we want to grow, we must train ourselves to begin at the end of the business process where the users are. From there, we must learn how to build backward in the hope of coming upon a business rather than building forward in the hope of coming upon a market. We must think inversely, starting "out there" where the profits are. If we start "in here," in our think tanks and laboratories, we start where only the costs are. The more we grow them, the less we profit.

A user's problem is a grower's profit. Problems, therefore, are the natural starting points for growth. Business growers must be problem seekers, problem analyzers, problem solvers—in short, problem thinkers.

The single key that can unlock growth opportunity is the simplistic question: *What is the problem?*

One of the reasons that growth is so rare is that we fail to ask markets what their problems are. We prefer to ask them to evaluate our solutions. Would you buy this?

If we can focus our thinking away from our own alleged solutions onto a market's actual problems, we can partner with our end users from the very inception of business. If we can remember that users share their problems but judge other people's solutions, we can enlist them openly in a cooperative effort. Together we can build the kind of solutions they will recognize as containing premium values because they have been the source for them. Users, in common with all of us, see their own contributions first and value them highest.

When we invert our growth strategy to work it backward, we start by getting into our users' heads. If we can get into their heads, we can get into their homes, their offices, their plants, their institutions, their services, and whatever else is germane to our growth quest. Once in, we can ask: *"What is the problem?"*

There are two types of problems we must look for. These will be the clues to our solutions:

1. *Problems that make a significant cost impact.* Customers are paying for their problems right now. Some problems run up direct costs. Other problems incur opportunity costs, depriving customers of money they could have if only they knew of a more cost effective way. There are also problems of the third kind that generate both types of costs. In each case, one of two things is true. Users have accurately quantified their costs or they have not. If they have, we must learn their numbers. If they have not, we must discover their numbers in partnership.

It may be technically possible to learn customers' numbers by ourselves, without them. But it is psychologically impossible to convince customers of the accuracy of our numbers unless they themselves have participated in their discovery.

Customer business functions that run up significant costs are the targets for growth businesses. Their values are the standards that must be exceeded by the values of our solutions. The premium nature of the price we can charge for our solutions will be directly proportional to the premium nature of the direct costs we reduce or the opportunity values we help achieve.

2. *Problems that make a significant sales impact.* Our customers, like us, live or die by sales. Many of them need greater volume. All of them can benefit from greater profits on their current volume. Most of them can benefit from new sources of profitable volume. The more profits we can help them make on what they sell, the more profits we can make on what they buy from us.

Customers have two types of sales problems. We can help with both. One is the improvement of their profits from sales to current markets. Can we help them sell more competitively by adding value to their products and to their selling strategy that will help them command a premium price? Can we help them sell more cost effectively, reducing their cost of sale or increasing its productivity? The second way we can help is by the improvement of customer profits from sales to new markets. Can we help them penetrate more cost effectively? Can we help them compete more aggressively by giving them the capability to price at a premium?

Can we, in short, act as *sales developers for our key customers?* In order to answer yes, we must possess two types of knowledge. We must know our customers' markets—who they sell to and how. And we must know the markets of our customers' customers—who they sell to and how. Customer sales development differs from customer cost reduction because it is a two-phase strategy. Unlike cost control, which is internal to our customers' operations, sales development is entirely external; first to our customers' markets and then to the markets of the customers of our customers.

Whether we select customer cost problems or sales problems, they share the same common denominator. Each must be quantified before we can know what the problem is. Problems whose solutions are the foundation for growth businesses are never mere narrative statements. They must always be expressed in numbers: dollars of costs or dollars of lost or unrealized sales.

A problem that is not quantified does not exist. A problem whose quantification is not significant to the customer does not exist as the basis for a growth solution.

Thinking Minimally

A grower's greatest temptation is to think big: a big business, a big market, big product lines that offer big benefits. Much of the time, bigness mitigates against growth.

If maximum profit is our objective, we must ask ourselves minimizing-type questions: What is the smallest business that will achieve our objectives? What is the smallest investment required to get such a business up and running? What is the smallest market share, the smallest product line, the smallest number of distribution channels, and the smallest sales force that will get us where we want to go?

Not how big must we be but how little? Not how many customers must we serve with how many lines of business but how few? These are the minimalist issues we must learn to deal with and the minimalist vocabulary in which we must learn to think. Otherwise our growth runs the risk of being unaffordable, unmarketable, and unprofitable.

Where growth is concerned, cost kills. It is commonplace for many growing businesses to be undercapitalized. But many more are overcosted from their inception, insuring the insufficiency of their initial financing.

Like Picasso, we may first work forward to fill our canvas. Then, through what he called a series of "progressive destructions," we can work backward to erase everything that is not essential to our objective. What is left should be our minimal daily growth requirement.

The correlation of a minimal business with maximized profits may, at first, seem paradoxical. On reflection, how could it be otherwise: Could a cost-heavy business ever maximize a growth market's profit opportunity? As our growth businesses move up their life-cycle curves toward maturity, we feel the effect immediately. The market opportunity is becoming saturated, we say. What we do not say is that our business cost structure is becoming saturated too.

The principle of "enoughness" underlies minimal thinking. Every business has its critical mass, the amount of resources that is enough from which to grow. Exceeding the critical mass is not only unproductive; it is also destructive. It makes it unnecessary to think centrically about the key pressure points of the business. Passively if not actively, it licenses flirtations with nonessentials and frivolities.

How much is *enough?* It is always the smallest amount necessary, never the largest. But necessary for what? Enoughness in a new business is the smallest investment necessary to maximize return. Enoughness in a new product is the smallest number of benefits necessary to command maximum price. Enoughness in a new market is the smallest number of heavy profit contributors whose cumulative contributions will add up to our business growth objectives.

Once we break the imaginary relationship in most of our minds between a maximized business and maximized profits, we can get comfortable with the fact that minimizing is the companion of optimizing. Whatever works to improve market profits and productivity is the beginning of a growth product line. Its lowest level of contribution may be called adequate. If no customer can match it and if no competitor can match it or exceed it, we can say that adequacy is sufficient for branding—that is, to merit premium price. If our contribution is in danger of becoming inadequate because of customer or competitor dynamics, we can add to it until it is adequate again—that is, until it can continue to command premium price.

In the meantime, we must learn to resist trading off what is already good enough for what may be better. In many growth businesses, better turns out to be the enemy of good enough by adding to it undesirable complexity and unaffordable cost. This may increase users' internal operating costs—their so-called hidden expenses—as well as their direct costs, thereby negatively altering the value-to-price relationship on which premium price depends. When this point is reached, the rate of decay underlying the business growth curve will inevitably accelerate.

Minimal thinkers find reassurance in the beliefs that maximum profits come from minimalized businesses and that adequate benefits are sufficient to warrant premium price points. By minimizing their business investment, they help insure their ability to control the business.

They also aid their concentration on the key issues of the business since they permit few other considerations to even come into being, let alone make distracting demands.

Thinking Preemptively

Managers who, sitting up at night, plan to make their businesses competitive against rival organizations plan for the wrong eventuality. Growth businesses cannot ignore competition. But they must define it differently. A growth business competes first and foremost against its customers' current solutions to significant problems. What are the costs they are incurring by living with these problems—can we reduce or eliminate them? What are the costs of their solutions—can we improve their return on investment even at a high or higher price? What are the opportunity costs of their lost sales potential—can we help them capture it?

Growth businesses rise or fall on their ability to compete against their customers' standard solutions. These solutions may range from doing nothing to using another supplier's products, services, and systems. But it is not other suppliers who must be competed against. Instead, it is the profit currently being earned by the customers. Can we improve their profit contributions significantly enough to earn the customers' attention? If so, and if we can prove it, we can supersede rival suppliers whose products help account for the customers' current profits.

Can we improve customer profit faster? Can we improve it with greater certainty? If so, we can sell by competing against the customer's existing bottom line without ever having to encounter other suppliers on a one-to-one basis.

Many managers, perhaps most, are not experienced in thinking of customers as competitors. When it comes to our growth, that is what customers are. To get their business, we must be able to do something for them that they cannot do as well, or do at all, for themselves: grow their own businesses.

To accelerate our growth, we must preempt our markets' perception of us as their principal partner in growth. We must brand ourselves as their premium supplier of added profit values.

Branding our role as growers—not growers of our own business, which is self-serving, but of our customer businesses—must become the core of our sales strategy. It enables our customers to prefer us as business partners and to be able to justify their preference. At the same time, it permits us to establish and maintain our rationale for premium pricing. As long as we can improve customer profits at an adequate margin over our price, price will become less and less decisive as a buying drive. In many cases, it will disappear completely from relevance.

Growth businesses are wholly dependent on brands. Without brands, there is no strategy for growing our customer profits or for preempting customer preference as their superior growth partner. Without brands, too, there is no strategy for earning premium profits through premium pricing. Without brands, no one grows: neither we nor our customers.

Thinking preemptively means planning to enter a growth market positioned to seize the branded role of the superior profit improver. We may or may not have the technically superior product. We do not need it. Our product must only be adequate. But we must have the superior market information database. We must also have the ability to sell from it in a way that quantifies the added values we can bring to solving customer cost problems and achieving customer sales opportunities.

If we are going to preempt the preference of a market, we must gain more than acceptance for our role. Acceptance is our entry barrier. Hurdling it, we gain access to the playing field. But entry is not preemption. Nor is access the equivalent of growth, which requires preference rather than acceptance. There are likely to be several categories of solution on the market at the same time: premature solutions, mature solutions that are stable and others that are in decline, and brands. To enter a market with anything but a brand is to relinquish growth because we will be unable to obtain preference.

The role of "acceptable alternate supplier" is the commodity-maker's role. It is as good as he or she is likely to get. Growers must seize the high ground as *the single preferred partner in profit improvement*. There is no room to share this role with other suppliers. It can only be shared in partnership with customers.

Thinking Pithily

To get to the pith of growth, we must 80-20 everything: 80-20 is the growers' verb. It must be applied to the invention process, to markets, to product lines, and to staff.

The 20 is the 20 percent of what we do that accounts for up to 80 percent of the profits from our business. The 20 is the profit-maker. The 80, the 80 percent of what we do that accounts for the remaining 20 percent or less of our profits, is composed of no-growth or slow-growth lines of business. Eighty percent type thinking is off-limits to growers. Price competition, purchasing agent decision-makers, bids, price-performance sales strategies, deals, and discounts are 80 percent sales strategies. They are noxious to the growth process.

"What is the 20 percent that will get us the 80 percent?" This is the branded business grower's quest. Whatever fits the answer becomes the grower's priority. Whatever does not fit becomes excess baggage.

Once in hand, the 20 percent drives the business. Twenty percent of the market provides the key-account customer base. Twenty percent of the products provides the most profitable sales volume. Twenty percent of the sales force brings the major profits home. Twenty percent of the development cycle for new products goes 80 percent of the way to determining their success. Twenty percent of a growth plan's strategies predict its profitability.

Insofar as possible, the world of 20 percent should be the universe. This argues for minimal strategies, lean plans, sparsely populated growth teams, and vertically segmented markets. Twenty percent thinking is not thinking small. It is thinking tight, thinking narrow.

Because growth rests on such a narrow base, it is easy to see why it is so precarious. It is hard to spread the risk. Anything that goes wrong with the 20 percent places growth in immediate jeopardy. There is no salvation to be found in tinkering with any of the 80 percent, although it is almost irresistibly tempting to try. Either the 20 percent works or growth will be unlikely.

Twenty percent thinking will focus our mind-sets on two of the most potent keystones to growth: the growth organization and the growth sales force together with its strategies.

1. *Organization intensity.*   Growth businesses are most vulnerable where they are most intensive. This is where their dependencies are. It is also where their costs are clustered. If our mission is to grow a technology-intensive business, the 20 percent of our thinking that will add 80 percent of the value will be on the management of our technical invention process and its commercialization into successive product launches at premium prices. For all intents and purposes, this is "the business." Similarly, the 20 percent of a labor-intensive business will be recruitment, training, and compensation. A distribution-intensive business requires a concentration on maximizing the advantages of retail location, promotion, and vertical market specialization.

Business intensity predetermines the subject matter of our thinking intensity. We can never relax. We must keep trying to find new ways to make the intensive focal points of our business more cost effective. If that slips away from us, and it will if our focus fuzzes, three things are certain. Costs will rise in our heaviest cost areas, our effectiveness will fall, and our rate of growth will slow.

2. *Sales strategy intensity.*   Sales strategies are the flip side of cost intensity. They are where the earnings are. The 20 percent of our

thinking that will add 80 percent of the value will be on new and improved ways of implementing our Consultative Selling strategies at the top tiers of our key customer accounts. Any way that will increase our yield per customer and decrease our cost of obtaining it can accelerate our growth.

What 20 percent thinking really dictates is that we must be our own profit improvers. We must practice vigilance to keep costs down in the operation of our main intensity, whatever it may be. If they run away with us, they will take our growth with them. On the other hand, we must continually monitor the revenue-to-investment ratio of our key-account sales function. How much more revenue can we earn with the same investment? How much more investment would be required to improve our revenue return substantially enough to make it worthwile? What strategies should we invest in?

For every growth business, just as for every customer business our growth business may hope to grow, growth thinking must focus on the numerator and denominator of our bottom line. How do we raise our profits from sales? How do we lower the operating costs that our sales require? In the answers we give, we either solve or compound the enigma of our growth.

11
Slowth

It is easy to identify a growth business. It is busy growing. It is deeply involved in an overt collaboration with its customers to grow them. It is equally easy to tell a no-growth or slow-growth business. It is busy debating growth. It is preoccupied with its own profits and the profits of its competitors, not its customers. It is transfixed by the costs of growth rather than their return. It asks, "What can we grow?" meaning which products, instead of "Who can we grow?" meaning which markets.

Growth businesses have growth to point to. They can document their commitment. Nongrowth businesses have other things to point to: growth principles, growth committees, and growth controls. They show additional clues as well. Ten of these signs of "slowth," the opposite of growth, are equally distributed among static or declining businesses.

1. *Declaration of principles.* A business that writes and rewrites a declaration of principles and then hangs them on its walls is not a growth business. There is only one growth principle: grow your customers. This is a full-time occupation. Any time spent in thinking up or writing down more principles detracts from growth. A business that devotes its time to growing customers has no time to do anything else.

2. *Hierarchy of objectives.* A business that debates or debases the primacy of profit as its superior objective is not a growth business. Profit is the sole criterion of growth; it is the substance of growth, the stuff of which growth is made as well as measured. Without profit, no other objectives are achievable. A business that is embarrassed to put profit first or is coy about admitting that it does is undeserving of growth.

3. *Preoccupation with risk.* A business that emphasizes the risk of

growth instead of its rewards is not a growth business. Risk-aversion constrains growth; reward subversion prevents it entirely. Growth businesses contemplate the rewards of growth far more than its risks. The ultimate risk is not to grow, to accept the opportunity cost of stasis or decline. A business that concentrates on foreshortening its reach will foreshorten its growth.

4. *Dispersion of resources.*   A business that puts an egg in every basket, rather than many eggs in few baskets, is not a growth business. Growth is the result of concentration, not dispersion. Scattered resources excuse management's dereliction in doing sufficient homework on its fewest, best opportunities. As a result, losers are fertilized and winners are starved. A well-rounded balance strategy is less conducive to growth than a pointed, unbalanced approach. A business that tries to grow with rounded strategies invites rounded results, in zeros.

5. *Organization by matrix.*   A business that is organized as a matrix is not a growth business. Matrix is the antithesis of growth. In order to grow, growth must have a single responsible leader who can command resources, direct their application, and administer reward and punishment. Leaderless growth is a contradiction in terms. A business that does not structure growth will not be restructured by it.

6. *Offices in cubicles.*   A business that houses managers in cubicles is not a growth business. Growth occurs either in small enclosed spaces like garages or in wide open unfettered spaces like fields or mountaintops. Anything in between inhibits growth because it lets in the extraneous, the intrusive, and the irrelevant. A business that does not stimulate its growers either with each other or with nature will not grow.

7. *Inappropriateness of models.*   A business that looks to mature multibillion-dollar corporations as growth models is not a growth business. Growth is a small-organization phenomenon: small teams, small resources, and small tight time frames. Small businesses are the only valid models of how to grow. "Three guys in a garage" is the only valid model of business development from scratch. A business that imitates invalid models will invalidate its growth.

8. *Acceptance of failure.*   A business that makes failure acceptable is not a growth business. Failed growth creates the precedent for more failed growth. Only successful growth must be acceptable in a growth business because growth teaches growth: Success is the model for continued success. If success is enforced, it will result. So will failure if it is permitted. A business that grows is a self-fulfilling prophecy.

9. *Apologies for culture.*   A business that acknowledges its culture as a handicap to growth is not a growth business. A no-growth or slow-

growth culture is a hostile medium. No business with such an affliction has the right to present a deficit as an opportunity—a challenge to be circumvented. Growth is a sufficient challenge. Time, energy, and resources devoted to circumvention detract from growth. A business that does not provide sails for its growers anchors them.

10. *Remoteness of management.* A business whose top management maintains a remoteness from growth is not a growth business. Growth policy originates at the top. Unless growth is a top-down process, it will not work. Management can induce growth but it cannot be induced to grow. Growers should not be required to waste time encouraging their management to grow; they should be encouraging their customers, who are the sources of their growth. A business with aloof management will always be distant from growth.

Index

About the Author

MACK HANAN is an international authority on business growth. Through his consulting firm, The Wellspring Group, he counsels Fortune 500 companies on how to grow their existing businesses and how to diversify into the growth businesses of the near future. He also works with entrepreneurial, high-technology start-up businesses to help them accelerate their growth. He is the inventor of expert systems for growth management and the author of several important books in the field, including *Venture Management, Accelerated Growth Planning*, and *High-Tech Growth Strategies*.